The Silent Conspiracy:
A Communist Model of Political Cleansing at the Slovak University in Bratislava after the Second World War

Zoltan G. Mesko, M.D.

EAST EUROPEAN MONOGRAPHS, BOULDER
DISTRIBUTED BY COLUMBIA UNIVERSITY PRESS, NEW YORK
2003

EAST EUROPEAN MONOGRAPHS, No. DCXVI

ISBN: 0-88033-514-9

Library of Congress Control Number: 2002115748

Printed in the United States of America

In memory of my beloved parents

Too old to carry arms and fight like the others –
they graciously gave me the inferior role of chronicler.
I record – I don't know for whom – the history of the siege.

Zbigniew Herbert

Contents

Figures

Acknowledgements

This story reveals a dramatic moment in time, shrouded in the mists of a raging and convoluted epoch. Sealed in a mysterious flask and thrown into a vast ocean far from the shores of judgement, after fifty years of drifting, the time capsule found its way home to my native country, Slovakia. From its folds of parchment appears a tale of covert times which touches present-day Slovakia, after the fall of the Berlin Wall. The actors of those bygone years, having played their roles as victors who succeeded in crushing their victims, now stand unmasked, no longer hidden by the curtains of time.

Years of thorough historical research would have been unthinkable without the extraordinary help of Mrs. Judy Weinstein, head of St. Francis Library in Roslyn, New York. At her desktop computer she participated in the hunt for dust-covered and yellowing monographs and documents. She has my everlasting gratitude and fond memories of our informal "morning briefs."

The victimized and defeated, who suffered immeasurably throughout those long and difficult years, also helped. It was privilege to listen to the testimony and confessions of five professors of the Medical School of the Slovak University who are still alive. Softened by their age and wisdom, and without any desire for revenge, they bared their souls to me.

In additions, the wives, sons and immediate relatives of six deceased professors also gave their testimony, as well as access to important documents from the Medical School in Bratislava and Košice. Documents from the civil authorities, the courts and the police, revealed the persecution of their beloved fathers, culminating in their professional and personal ruin. Despite their ordeal, none of the living professors or their relatives lost their personal, professional or patriotic convictions. Only one family of one former professor declined to participate in this historic retrospection.

Many of my colleagues, now in retirement, were willing to reveal previously unknown information, exhibiting precious yellowing documents which detailed their demise and mirrored the times and society which followed the victorious February "Putsch" of the Communists in 1948 and the period of the so-called "democratization" of the University. All information was carefully collected, reviewed, and corroborated by various sources and was used only if factual and in accordance with actual events. All personal impressions were left out. To all the aforementioned, my thanks. Their testimonies and evidence served as my compass and revealed the landscape of this treacherous period.

In the years following 1990 a group of historians from Slovakia showed significant interest in this story. They viewed it as a model of political cleansing which occurred, not only at the Medical School, but in other institutions as well. Their contributions, discussions and keen critique were priceless reflections of their professional expertise and for this I am deeply grateful. The graphic art and cover were created by my daughter Patricia. She was also my first editor and critic. Her unfading interest, suggestions and inspiration helped me to accomplish my work. My special thanks go to Mr. Mark Stolarik, Professor and Chairholder of the Chair in Slovak History at the University of Ottawa, for his exceptional interest and belief that my story should be made public, as well as for his kind review and editorial assistance.

An old proverb says it best, "Behind every remarkable man, there is a remarkable woman." The ultimate laurel belongs to my wife, Judith, who listened to my youthful memoirs and reflections and read through the rough draft during its fermentation. I imposed upon her never-ending patience and tolerance, even in the silence of the night, when I lit a flashlight in order to capture the evanescent thoughts which awoke me. For her unending help, understanding and devotion, as well as her belief in the sense and importance of my literary toil and mission, I remain forever grateful.

Zoltan G. Mesko

Preface

In summer of 1999 a slim but interesting-looking book arrived in my mail with the curious Slovak title of *Zamlčané sprísahanie* (The Silent Conspiracy). Intrigued by the title. I started leafing through it and discovered that I could not put it down. Here, finally was an exposé, by an insider, of how the Communists had infiltrated, deformed and degraded the Faculty at the Medical School of the Slovak (Comenius) University in Bratislava, Czechoslovakia, as well as its sister University of P. J. Šafarik in the eastern metropolis of Košice. Much worse, here was detailed description of how the best physicians in Slovakia had their careers (and many times their lives) destroyed by their Communist colleagues in the 1940's and 1950's. the net result was the severe deformation of medical science in Slovakia, a deformation from which it has not yet recovered.

Unfortunately, Dr. Mesko's books was written in Slovak and therefore it was originally only available to a limited group of readers. I believed that it should reach a much wider audience and encouraged him to translate it into English, which he did. I was happy to contribute by reviewing his text and editing it, as well as by writing an overview of Slovak history in the first chapter in order to put his story into its proper context. Readers of this book should keep in mind that Zoltan G. Mesko is not a historian, nor does he pretend to be. However, he has an important story to tell, from first-hand experience eof destructiveness, immorality and depravity of certain Slovak Communists and it is a story that should not wait for professional historians. By the time they get around to telling it, the perpetrators of many despicable actions revealed by Dr. Mesko will have long departed this word.[1] Sadly, some of them (or their disciples) are still held in high esteem in post-Communist Slovakia and some of them are trying to block the transformation of Slovak society and its institutions from a totalitarian to a democratic model. They need to be exposed and removed from their ill-gotten positions if Slovakia is ever to attain parity with its western European neighbors.

M. Mark Stolarik
Professor and Chairholder
Chair in Slovak History and Culture
University of Ottawa, Canada

Dr. Zoltan G. Mesko

Bratislava, May 21, 1950. Czechoslovakia

Comrade Ernest Sykora, Secretary of Education (in Slovakia):

"We can't have professors at the University who have sympathies only for the new political order, socialist science and socialism. We have to have people who will build a bastion of Marxism-Leninism and be involved in the moral struggle against the remnants of the reactionary bourgeoisie and religion!"

Pravda (The Truth),
Bratislava, 1950: 31:3, No. 118.

Introduction

The noted Canadian physiologist Hans Selye, who at the beginning of the twentieth century spent his early childhood in southern Slovakia, conceptualized the theory of stress at a rather early age. Reflecting on protracted intellectual fermentation, Selye followed with the discovery of this astounding thesis that changed our thinking and lives in many ways. In one of his popular texts, entitled "How to become a Scientist," Selye mused that during this mental procreation he felt like being in a state of intellectual gestation or pregnancy. Years of precious time and the accumulation of individual building blocks were necessary to bring about this point of critical mass to the resolution of this fortuitous design. At the end of it, at long last, he felt that the task was accomplished and that he was ready for intellectual presentation or delivery.

A moment of tremendous relief and elation followed when Selye grasped that he ad accomplished this tortuous journey and was certain he could reveal his original findings to the scientific world. He compared his feelings at this poignant moment to the bliss and felicity of a mother who, after a taxing gestation, delivered her beautiful baby. Selye mused, "We men are, of course, deprived of these unique and blessed feelings after such an intense accomplishment. We can perhaps only fathom such relief and satisfaction after a much more prosaic mammalian decompression."[1]

I read Selye's text to medical students in 1947 as a first-year tender in Medical School and it made a memorable impression on me. I did not know then what tumultuous political events would consequently occur—indeed a revolution—when in February of 1948, the democratic republic of Czechoslovakia was taken over by Moscow-indoctrinated and Prague-based Communists and "apparatchiks." It had a tremendous psychological impact on me to witness this brutal political act and its actors, these vulgar and crass proletarian copies of the Soviet superman. It culminated when the Medical School and its teachers were hit with a savage frontal attack by these Communist

1

lackeys at the University. Our best and most respected professors and our beloved Dean, for whom the students harbored great affection, were abruptly dismissed. These dramatic events planted a germ in my mind and heart and gave me the conviction that this story, which I witnessed, should be told.

The experience of this period pressed upon me and I mulled it over through that long intellectual gestation which Selye so poignantly described. This incubation period, during which my memories have crystallized, is now at the point of critical mass whereby these wrongdoings and miscarriages of justice are available for full exposure.

My journey to study medicine unfolded incrementally, coming about almost by default. I was a fairly good high school student and my parents had achievable expectations for my future and career. Having a technical background, my dad expected me to follow in his footsteps. But it soon became more than apparent in junior high that the fairy godmother of mathematics had not been present at my cradle. I drove my beloved dad apoplectic when I failed to understand the elementary logic in mathematical equations, despite the assistance of beautiful multicolored graphs and designs written in his delicate handwriting. I saw deep disappointment in his otherwise mischievous blue eyes and I felt terrible that I had let him down. However, he let me go, accepting my mother's sensible advice that I would mature and certainly catch up later.

At the same time, a biology teacher appeared on the scene of my chronicle. He was of peasant stock and looked less like a teacher of the early 1940's than a farmer. The gargantuan watch in his waist pocket, with its long and heavy golden chain was the trademark of his Samson-like chest. Despite his robust frame, he was of gentle spirit, very soft-spoken and an open-minded and inspiring teacher. In the mores of these years, homework was compulsory and a serious matter. During springtime, for biology class, every student had to adopt a tree or bush in his backyard and not only tend the ground and water it, but also observe how Mother Nature comes to life and sprouts her dormant buds and offshoots. Every morning at six o'clock I ran down to my bush with my shovel, bucket and calipers and then measured the size of the buds on the prelabeled twigs and put these daily measurements in length and width on an X and Y axis on a paper grid. As we compared the measurements in size versus time in our biology classes, from day one to the break of the first blossom, we were amazed by these new discoveries in growth and development.

At about the same time, I stumbled on a volume by Paul de Kruif, *The Microbe Hunters*. As an avid reader, I devoured the book and was fascinated by the research of Louis Pasteur, who discovered that microorganisms caused illnesses. Pasteur also developed the first vaccine against rabies to save a boy's life—this was all new and spellbinding information for me. The discovery by Robert Koch, the hunter of the ever-elusive tuberculosis bacillus, captivated me. His wife was instrumental in the isolation of this pale microbe, crippling the evasive bug with the sticky gelatin of her apricot preserves.

As a consequence of these readings, I reflected on and turned my interest towards the field of medicine and its unexpected wonders and secrets. My decision to study medicine was sealed when I encountered Martin Arrowsmith in the Sinclair Lewis novel. The clarity of approach of this protagonist during an epidemic of the plague, combined with his deep personal interest in human suffering and readiness to help under dire circumstances, made a deep impression on me and today is ever fresh. His further research using the microscope and ultracentrifuge and his discoveries at the Rockefeller Institute in New York were so inspiring that I decided to go "my way." Never did I fathom in the mid-1940's that I would one day in the future be in New York adjacent to this temple of science attending a medical conference at Cornell.

A year after I graduated with honors from high school, my mother was proud that her only son made the choice to become a physician. In 1947 I applied to the Medical School in Bratislava, a choice which I never regretted. To my great happiness and excitement I was accepted for the fall semester.

However, we were financially strapped on my late father's pension. Furthermore, two years after the Second World War and its devastation, there was an extreme shortage of lodging in the capital. Fortunately, my mom was a strong and resourceful woman and, after some asking around, she turned to our parish priest. Having known my family for years, Father John responded, "I'll see what I can do." A few weeks later I received a message: "Go and see the Abbot of the Dominican order. He would like to meet you." I prepared by dressing my best and rang at the Abbey at the appointed time. The Abbot, a burly middle-aged man in a black and white cassock, with curly salt-and-pepper hair and penetrating eyes the color of a hazelnut, gave me a hearing regarding my problem. He finally discharged me with a brusque remark, "I will let you know."

In late summer a letter arrived stating that I had been accepted by the dormitory of Saint Svorad (nicknamed "Svoradov" by the students) in Bratislava. I was also given a stipend covering all expense. I was report to the dorm on September 25, 1947. I was both overjoyed by this news and in anguish as well since I had dearly cherished my home life and now had to leave. In addition, I hadn't the faintest clue as to who Saint Svorad was. In our *Encyclopedia* at home I discovered he was a Benedictine monk who spread the news of Christianity near the ancient city of Nitra, which had been the seat of bishops of Slovakia since the Middle Ages.

As requested, I reported to the dorm in late September. Because of the housing shortage after the Second World War, most of the rooms had to be shared. I was lucky to be assigned to a room with a senior medical student who expected to be alone in his quarters prior to his graduation exams. To his unconcealed displeasure, he ended up with a greenhorn and an extra cot. Fortunately, Joseph was a very decent man and took me under his wing. We remained friends ever since.

The dorm was established in the early thirties for Catholic university students. The whole complex served about 300 students from all over Slovakia and was built mostly from donations by the faithful. It was a rather large rectangular fortress, with a central courtyard and a large gym for fitness activities. It housed a nice library as well and spacious lecture rooms for conferences. Sublime and ever-smiling Vincentian nuns tended a huge kitchen and dining room. The nuns also cared for the beautiful chapel with its altar decorated by a center-piece of Byzantine mosaics that portrayed the crucified Christ. The corridors of the dormitories connected to the choir and in the silence of the chapel students could pray or unwind in meditation between studies.

Our daily regimen was rather Spartan. Each morning we left for the Medical School to attend courses; we broke for a bit to eat during the noon recess and returned to the dorms by dusk. After supper, at eight o'clock, silence was in order, followed by rigorous cramming and preparations through the advanced hours of the night until dawn. Coming from an intellectual middle-class family, from the cosmopolitan city of Košice, I found myself slightly at odds with the students from mostly simple and rather humble backgrounds who came from small towns as well as from the countryside. These students were the beloved sons of farmers, small shopkeepers and tradesmen, as well as manual or blue-collar working families. It was notable right away that the members of this student body did not have an easy youth and studied very hard and took this opportunity and privilege for a higher education very seriously. It should be said that for this avant-garde there was no charge for room and board and after the war, this was a major contribution to any student's budget and life.

I was on the shy side but nevertheless blended well with these friendly chaps who at the same time were fun-loving and had a good sense of humor. They recognized and appreciated their hard-earned and privileged positions. With the help of their church and country there was the expectation that they would become the elite of their society. I soon sensed as well that they cherished a profound national pride and had a great respect and love for their roots, nation and land while I differed from them as I lacked these genes.

These were difficult and worrisome years and although I was very much immersed in my medical studies, I still had an inkling from the discussions around me by the students who were history majors that tumultuous and difficult political times lay ahead. After the Second World War, Slovakia's political situation war rather complicated. On the one hand, the Slovak national uprising in August 1944 against the occupying Germans and their collaborators helped the Slovaks redeem themselves and end up on the victorious side of the war. On the other hand, the Slovaks also had to face the political repercussions having had, in 1939 after the Munich Agreement and under Hitler's ultimatum, declared their own interwar Republic as the only practical option to preserving their nationhood and salvaging their land. More importantly, after the Yalta conference in February 1945, Czechoslovakia fell into the Soviet orbit and Dr. Edvard Beneš, the leader of postwar Czechoslovakia, yielded to the Moscow-trained Czechoslovak Communists. He permitted them to become the dominant and decisive force that eventually led to his downfall and condemned his country to Soviet dominion.

I learned from my roommate Joseph the outcome of these political tensions and changed which came about immediately after the end of the war. A large number of Slovak university professors were expelled from the Medical School and the whole university. This elite group of intellectuals was the first "homegrown" generation of Slovak professors who had established their academic credentials before the war, that is, during the first Czechoslovak Republic (1918–1938). They were the "crème de la crème" of the nation.

These professors had remained active in the Medical School during the Slovak Republic (1939–1945) as teachers, educators and scholars. They were absolutely necessary for running the highest schools of the country and, as a consequence of having served their nation during this precarious time, they carried the blemish of guilt by association. According to Joseph, their liabilities were that, as genuine Slovaks, they did not subscribe to the concept of the "Czechoslovak nation"—a banner on which the first Republic had been deceptively established. Instead, they were disciples of the heritage of their own distinct nationhood and aspired for its autonomous governance. Most of all, as representatives of the majority of their nation, they were almost all practicing Catholics. This was a major liability in postwar Eastern European societies that were involuntarily assigned to Soviet control.

Joseph sincerely lamented the abrupt dismissal of his respected teachers, which had not been based upon their professional failure, but was retribution for their different political and religious beliefs. They were swiftly replaced by associates who espoused the ideology of "Czechoslovakism," and were also members of the Protestant minority in Slovakia. These men aspired to reclaim their privileged positions in the first Republic. Many of them were influential leftists, and in some instances, either had outright Communist credentials or were soon to become Communists. It was under the new Minister of Education, the journalist and Communist poet Ladislav Novomeský, himself a former Protestant, where the political plot and dismissal of the university physicians was orchestrated.

These political changes and retribution at the University, as well as the progress of Communism, were of great concern to the students at Svoradov. As Catholic students of a predominantly Catholic nation, they had great reservations against the rising Marxist-Leninist ideology and its proxies with totalitarian credentials.

In the spring of 1946, during the last free and democratic elections of postwar Czechoslovakia, the whole student body of the dorm demonstrated in favor of the Slovak Democratic Party. Their demonstration attracted thousands of citizens, supporters and sympathizers who gather together before the dormitory. The leading students called upon the citizens to guard the democratic principles of freedom and warned against the ascendancy of the totalitarian Communist forces and their infiltration of the government, media, police and security forces. The demonstration, while peaceful, was disrupted when a truckload of Communists attacked the students and large crowd of people, assaulting them with rocks. Shots were fired into the crowd and about a dozen people were injured.

I listened with considerable skepticism to these incidents and, despite my own fears, burrowed myself more deeply into my studies of biology and the chromosomes of the Mediterranean fruit fly. It was unlikely that Joseph was trying to impress with this information. However, there was an uneasy feeling among the freshmen that we were going to face some dramatic events.

Six months later, at the beginning of the second semester in February of 1948, all hell broke loose. The Moscow-indoctrinated Communist ministers in the central government cornered the vacillating Czechoslovak President and, with an organized coup d'état, took control of the government. Never did we dream that this Communist zealotry, this spiritual darkness, would last over forty years and would bring with it such political, economic, cultural and moral devastation, combined with the total overhaul and social engineering of every human stratum of this once mostly Catholic and conservative society.

1
Proscenium in History – The Slovaks

By M. Mark Stolarik
Chair in Slovak History and Culture
University of Ottawa

Although the Slovaks, a small nation (pop. 5,300,000) in the heart of Central Europe now live in their own (since 1993) Slovak Republic, they had to struggle for over 1,5000 years to achieve an independent existence. Ruled by foreigners for over a millennium, the Slovaks were buffeted by the tides of history and their culture reflects this diversity. Today they are struggling to assert their presence on the European, and world, stage.

The ancestors of the Slovaks arrived in Central Europe in the tumultuous 5th and 6th centuries, after the collapse of the Roman Empire. Like other Slavs, they moved into the vacuum left by the departing German tribes, who moved west and south. The Slovaks settled permanently in the shadow of the High and Low Tatra Mountains and in the valleys of the Váh, Hron and Hornád Rivers, which drain the northern arc of the Carpathian Mountains and flow into the might Danube River. In the 7th century they enjoyed a brief independence from the Asiatic Avars in the Empire of Samo (630–658), and full independence in the Great Moravian Empire (833–906).[1]

The latter would leave a lasting impression upon the Slovaks because in 863 the Greek missionaries, Sts. Cyril and Methodius, came to convert the Slovaks to Byzantine Christianity. Although the Slovaks joined the Eastern Christian world in the 9th century, Roman Catholicism predominated in the 10–11th centuries because the Asiatic Magyars conquered the Slovaks at that time and the new rulers accepted Christianity from Rome.[2]

For the next 1,000 years the Slovaks lived in the Kingdom of Hungary and shared its fate. The Magyar rulers built mighty fortresses along the northern frontier with Poland, many of which still exist

(Budatín in Žilina, Oravský zámok in Orava, L'ubovna in Spiš and Zborov in Šariš). These fortresses also testified to the feudal order that prevailed in Hungary until the revolution of 1848. Since the Kingdom of Hungary was a multi-cultural society, its rulers selected Latin as the official language (until 1840), which minimized ethnic friction.[3]

When the Protestant Reformation came to Central Europe in the 16th century, the Slovaks became divided into Roman Catholics, Lutheran, Calvinists, and Greek Catholics. The Reformation brought with it the first translation of the Bible into Slovakized Czech (the Slovaks had not yet codified their own language), and the first religious and secular tracts, also written in Slovakized Czech. The Jesuits, who came to Slovakia in the early 17th century to lead the Counter-Reformation, established the first Catholic universities on Slovak territory in the western city of Trnava (1635–1777) and in the eastern metropolis of Košice (1657–1777). Under the influence of the Jesuits, most Slovaks (about 80%) became Roman Catholics again; 15% were Lutheran and the rest were Greek Catholics or Calvinists.[4]

During the Enlightenment of the 18th century the Slovak language was finally codified but this divided the Slovaks even more. In 1787 the Roman Catholic priest Anton Bernolak (1762–1813) codified the cultured western Slovak that had been used at the University of Trnava before Emperor Joseph II moved that institution to Budapest. Unfortunately, Slovak Protestants, who had been using Slovakized Czech as their liturgical language since the 16th century, refused to use the new codification and Slovak intellectuals now wrote in both western Slovak (Roman Catholics) and in Slovakized Czech (Lutherans).[5]

This division reflected another disagreement among Slovak intellectuals—the question of whether the Slovaks were a distinct nation or part of the Czech (or Czechoslovak) nation. The Czechs lived in the Austrian part of the Empire and spoke a language that was close to (but not the same as) Slovak. The Roman Catholics insisted that the Slovaks were a distinct nation whereas the Lutherans tended to view themselves as part of the "Czechoslovak" nation. This split among the Slovak intellectuals occurred during the most dangerous part of their history—when the ruling Magyars of Hungary decided to try to turn the multi-cultural Kingdom of Hungary into a Magyar

Kingdom, where all ethnic groups had to assimilate into the Magyar language and culture.[6]

Perceiving the folly of writing in two codifications, the Lutheran teacher L'udovit Stúr (1815–1856) decided to solve the problem. In 1843 he re-codified Slovak, based on central Slovak dialects, and persuaded fellow Lutheran, as well as the Roman Catholics, to follow suit. In 1851 both sides accepted the new codification and since then most intellectuals have written in what became standard Slovak.[7]

Even though the linguistic problems that had plagued the Slovaks were resolved at mid-century, political problems continued to bedevil them. The Magyars continued in their efforts to forcibly assimilate the Slovaks in the second half of the 19th century and Slovak leaders were divided in their response. A minority accepted assimilation and urged their countrymen to follow suit. The majority of Slovak intellectuals, however, went in other directions. The largest group, headquartered in the central Slovak town of Turčiansky Svätý Martin, looked to Russia to rescue the Slovaks from the clutches of the Magyars. A smaller group, who were studying at the Czech Charles IV University in Prague, and who became ardent followers of the professor of philosophy, T. G. Masaryk (1850–1937), resurrected the earlier philosophy of "Czechoslovakism" and hoped to create a new state of the Czechs and Slovaks if the opportunity arose.[8]

World War I (1914–1918) afforded the Czechs and the Slovaks the occasion to escape their oppressors in Austria-Hungary and to create a republic of their own. Shortly after the war broke out, T. G. Masaryk fled to the west to try to achieve his dream. He found support among Czech and Slovak immigrants in the United States who had met in Cleveland on October 22, 1915, and had agreed to join forces in the struggle to liberate their countrymen back home and to create a new, federated, state of the Czechs and Slovaks. Unfortunately for the Slovaks, Masaryk was an ardent "Czechoslovak" who refused to accept the Cleveland Agreement that had promised the Czechs and the Slovaks complete equality in the proposed new state. Therefore, Masaryk drafted a new agreement in Pittsburgh on May 30, 1918, in which the Czechs and Slovaks agreed to create a new Czech-Slovak Republic, but he left out the word "federation." He only implicitly promised the Slovaks home-rule with provisions that the Slovaks would have their own Diet (Parliament), their own courts, schools, and the use of the Slovak language.[9]

At the end of World War I Austria-Hungary collapsed and Czecho-Slovakia came into being with the support of the victorious Allies. (Fig. 1.1) Unfortunately for the Slovaks, Masaryk repudiated the Pittsburgh Agreement and Czechoslovakia became a unitary state without the hyphen, with the majority Czechs ruling over the minority Slovaks. Slovak Roman Catholics, by and large, were outraged, whereas most Slovak Lutherans supported the new arrangement. Slovak Catholics, led by the Rev. Andrej Hlinka (1864–1938) of the Slovak People's Party, agitated for the next twenty years for the implementation of the Pittsburgh Agreement (with the support of most American and Canadian Slovaks).[10]

The Slovaks finally achieved their long-sought home-rule in 1938 and 1939, but under most unfortunate circumstances. The Nazi dictator Adolph Hitler (1889–1945) set out to destroy Czechoslovakia and, after the Munich Pact of September 28–29, 1938, when the Allies abandoned Czechoslovakia to its fate, the Slovaks once again demanded home-rule and on October 6th the Czechs finally granted it. The new, federated Czecho-Slovakia lasted only until March 14, 1939, when the Slovaks, urged on by Hitler, declared independence. Since the Slovak Republic was allied with Germany, it lasted only until 1945, when Germany went down in defeat.[11]

After the Second World War the Slovaks faced several additional setbacks. Because the victorious Allies re-united Czechoslovakia in the spring of 1945, the Slovaks lost their home-rule and fell first under Czech, and in 1948, under Communist rule as well. In 1968 the Slovaks managed to regain a federated Republic during the reform rule of the Slovak Communist Alexander Dubček (1921–1993) and his "Prague Spring," but it was all dashed by the Soviet-led invasion of August 21, 1968. After that, until Communism collapsed in Czechoslovakia in November of 1989, the Slovaks were once again ruled by a centralized Communist bureaucracy based in the Czech capital of Prague.[12]

In 1990 the Czechs and Slovaks again debated their destiny. The Czechs, led by the former dissident playwright Václav Havel (b. 1937), who had been appointed president of the Republic in December, 1989, proposed to merely change the name of their

Republic from the previous Czechoslovak Socialist Republic to the Czechoslovak Republic. The Slovaks, on the other hand, wished to return the hyphen to Czecho-Slovakia, as it had been in 1918–1920 and 1938–1939. This disagreement about the name of their common state was symbolic of the deep differences between the Czechs and Slovaks regarding their future. The Czechs wished the centralized Republic to continue. The Slovaks wished to de-centralize it. Since they could not agree on their common future, they decided to divorce after their 68-year marriage. This finally happened on January 1, 1993, when both peoples went their separate ways in their own Republics.[13]

Fig. 1.1: Czecho-Slovakia, 1918–1938

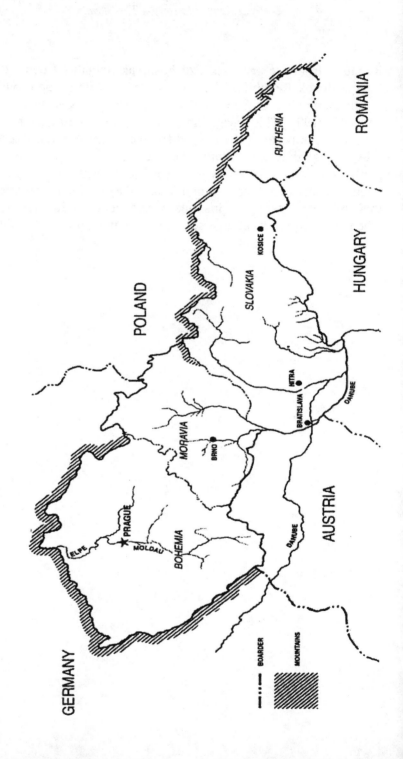

2
The University Between the Two Wars

The University as a temple of science and higher education was not only a faithful reflection of the advanced intellectual needs of society at all times but from the Middle Ages onwards its inner life was a true mirror of the religious, national and political dynamics of the society from which it was born. The universities of the 19th century were hotbeds of religious strife and nationalism, as was the case in nearby Prague, Budapest and Vienna. Even today the University remains the center of the struggle for self-realization, for ideological and political freedom and human rights against totalitarian regimes, as we saw in Tiananmen Square in 1989.

The University of Bratislava went through a difficult gestation and a traumatic birth from the time of its Hungarian inception in 1912 when it principally served the needs of the Hungarian kingdom. After the First World War, it changed both its nationality and spirit, along with the territories it served. In 1919 a Czechoslovak institution renamed Comenius University was sown into the intellectual soil of the Slovak national scene.

In its metamorphosis from being a Hungarian, then Czechoslovak and eventually a Slovak university, it mirrored the times reflecting the postwar establishment of Czecho-Slovakia and its political hegemony. As the clash of the Second World War overwhelmed Central Europe, the University echoed the national aspirations of this small nation and, despite the whirlwind of the Teutonic quest of *"Drang nach Osten,"* it grasped this opportunity to flourish during monstrous times. After the Allied victory a short period of academic freedom followed in what was hopefully a more just and politically balanced Czechoslovakia. However, Communism rolled over this geographic area with lasting consequences, dictating its totalitarian regime for the next forty years.

In 1912 the Austro-Hungarian Emperor Franz Joseph established the Elisabeth University in Pozsony (Hungarian for Bratislava) as the third university of the Hungarian Kingdom. This came about because the University in Budapest was overcrowded and Vienna was located a mere fifty miles from Bratislava, where one third of the student body originated from Hungary. The Emperor chose Pozsony, the coronation town of Hungary during the Ottoman wars, where eleven Habsburgs had been crowned in Saint Martin's Cathedral (1563-1830).[1] Lectures were expected to start in the fall of 1914 but instead of filling the classrooms, the lads were recruited for the trenches. The guns of August had started to fire.

Teaching started in the Medical School in the fall of 1918, after the end of the First World War. The Paris Peace Conference was still in the process of delineating the southeastern borders of the newly created Czecho-Slovakia, when on January 1, 1919, Czech troops and police, in cooperation with the French military, occupied Bratislava as part of the new Republic. By the summer of 1920 Bratislava's fate as the capital of Slovakia sealed was with the Treaty of Trianon.

At this time, while working in ambulatory clinics and striving to break into academia as a lecturer, Dr. Krystian Hynek, an ambitious and highly-educated forty-year-old Czech internist, discovered an article in a medical journal from the Department of Internal Medicine of the Elisabeth University of Pozsony (Bratislava).[2] Until that moment he had never heard of this institution. But he saw the political handwriting on the wall regarding the future of the city. It would fall into the lap of the new Republic and his own as well. Seeing the shortage of positions in the immediate future and the crowded conditions at the Charles IV University in Prague, Hynek seized this opportunity to make a quantum leap in his own career. He informed some of his younger associates from the ambulatory clinics about this potential opportunity. They had no information about the city or even knew its exact whereabouts, although leading Slovak medical historians Milan Beniak and Miroslav Tichý claim that Hynek's group "yearned to help the Slovaks and have a sincere relations with their people." It was the military, still in charge, which provided some information about the geography of the town, its hospitals and departments.[3]

Hynek knew that some political footwork had to be done in Prague since Rector Karol Pražak of Charles IV University was not keen on building satellite universities in the new Republic. Hynek cleverly used his political acquaintances, including T. G. Masaryk, the

President of the Republic, whose birthplace was about fifty miles west of Bratislava.[4] In May of 1919, eight doctors, headed by Krystian Hynek, traveled to Bratislava. The city was still studded with sentries and machinegun nests, and looked spooky and uninviting. To Hynek the town looked like a village and had the smell of Asia.[5]

Hynek's unannounced visit and his futuristic goals surprised the plenipotentiary minister to Slovakia, Dr. Vavro Šrobár, himself a physician, and his governmental body. Dr. Šrobár was initially disinclined to abolish the Hungarian University, being concerned with the Hungarian irredentists in a town where, at that time, Slovaks constituted only a small minority (15%).[6] However, Hynek was not a pushover and in his own interest he pressed on with well-prepared arguments that "his" University was in the Czechoslovak national and political interests, educating a new Slovak intelligentsia.[7] Hynek did not shy away from bluffing that the German branch of Charles IV University, with its faculty's allegiance to Germany, was expected to close. When his associates quipped that the President was watching, Dr. Šrobár quickly changed his original stance.[8]

The eventual meeting between the Hungarian and Czech professors was frosty and shortly afterwards the Hungarians were rounded up and interned.[9] The Hungarian rector failed to grasp the political reality and instead of the universality of their educational mission, blatant nationalism prevailed on both sides. Hynek made the conditions of remaining at the university unacceptable to the Hungarians, demanding that they swear allegiance to the new Republic. The Hungarians flatly refused, to Hynek's great relief.[10] Despite this clash, the heads of the departments eventually exchanged their positions and inventory in a dignified way. It was Hynek's great concern that the Hungarian University be officially shut down in order to avoid the appearance that the new Czechoslovak University was erected on the rubble of an old one.

Nevertheless, the new University was intending to utilize all of the physical plant of the hospital-based clinical departments with the exception of three large military barracks that the Hungarians had allotted for the basic science departments. These were retaken by the Czechoslovak army and created a significant impediment and spatial disadvantage for the new University.

Hynek and his group faced the enormous challenge of building a new University from scratch. By and large, they fulfilled this tremendous task in an exemplary way and left and indelible medical heritage and imprint on Slovakia's academic education and health care.

After Hynek was meritoriously elected as the first Rector and Chairman of the Department of Internal Medicine, the ten clinical department heads were appointed and their academic rank was automatically advanced to full professors. This occurred even though a few of them were still in Siberia in the medical service of the Czechoslovak legions.

Additional junior doctors were recruited from Prague as Assistant Professors and an entourage of Czech administrators came to face the managerial tasks of running the University. An estimated 200 doctors and officers subsequently arrived. The Czech leadership lacked interest and trust in the local professionals from Bratislava. The Slovaks were an enigma for these Czech newcomers. Only one Assistant Professor from the Elisabeth University, Dr. Joseph Dérer, an ophthalmologist, was employed. He was the youngest brother of Dr. Ivan Dérer, a politician and one of the few Slovaks totally devoted the Czechoslovak cause.

For the Czech professors, even under difficult conditions. This was a tremendous professional opportunity. This was virgin land with uncontested academic positions in comparison to the head-to-head rivalry in Prague. Nevertheless, most of the professors kept their eyes open for any chance to return to Charles IV University, and about a quarter of them did so in the not-too-distant future.[11]

The University had to be named. The choice was made in favor of Jan Amos Comenius, a 17th century Utraquist bishop from Moravia, who was known abroad for his work, *The Great Didactic*. Comenius was greatly admired by President Masaryk, whose wish as, therefore, granted. For the majority of the Slovaks, a nation made up of 70% Catholics, this was an insensitive choice—if not an outright affront—for the institution in their land. Naming the University after a man who meant nothing to them was perceived by some as a political smokescreen in order to humiliate the Slovaks.

In the fall of 1919, the first lectures for the clinical semesters and the 3rd, 4th, and 5th year started. Fortunately, a good hospital base was available while lack of lecture halls and administrative space caused grave problems. The student body was comprised of medical students from neighboring Vienna and Budapest and by Czech students. The Czech students were sent to strengthen the Czech element and maintain the Czechoslovak philosophy, as the University was to be Czechoslovak bastion.[12] In the first years, the preponderance of students was still Hungarian and German. The next year the Medical School was flooded by 150 Jewish students from Poland and Russia, comprising up to 50% of the student body until the late 1920's.[13] From 1930 on, the Slovaks and Czechs finally prevailed although a significant Hungarian and German minority was still present. This, of course, reflected the national composition of the city where in 1910 only about 15% of the citizens were of Slovak origin.

This mosaic of students with different native languages created an obstacle to effective communication and lectures. This was in important factor in these times since after the war textbooks were virtually unavailable. Copying the form and structure of the Charles IV University in Prague, all the lectures and administration of the Medical School were in Czech. After the students protested about the professors lecturing in Czech, understandable only to a small minority of Czechs and most Slovaks with some qualifications, the University agreed to summarize the lectures in German for the German and Jewish students, while the Hungarians were left out in the cold. The Czech professors were disinclined to lecture in Slovak and none of them made a sincere effort to lecture in that language. They regarded it a waste of time to develop a Slovak scientific language in what was a center of Czechoslovak thought. The Slovak students and the new graduates, of course, though otherwise.[14]

The need for housing for the professors, their associates and especially for the students created enormous problems that the political authorities failed to solve. Hynek miscalculated the amount of financial support coming from the central government in Prague. Having their own intelligentsia, the Czechs were not interested in fostering a Slovak one. The University in Bratislava was getting only one third of the financial support which the well-endowed Charles IV University in Prague was receiving. Hynek's repeated requests for 250 grants and stipends for the students went unheeded, despite vigorous student demonstrations.[15] This was a significant cause of discontent and furthermore planted the seeds of anti-Czech sentiment. Plans for a new University were made repeatedly, but for the entire twenty years of the first Czecho-Slovak Republic, nothing was built except for a small building for the basic sciences. Dorms were built or taken from religious sources. The Catholic dorm of Saint Svorad was established first in an old building and then in a newly rebuilt one. The Protestant students were mainly housed in the Štefánik House, and later in La Franconi, where they actually mixed together. A cleavage along religious lines evolved and translated itself into political allegiances whereby the Protestant students were more inclined to the state Czechoslovak persuasion.

As time went by, it became an urgent and almost indispensable measure for the Medical School to establish courses in the basic sciences in order to have a supply of medical students for the clinical semesters. This was accomplished by Hynek and the new associates who came from Prague.[16] They were led by the energetic Zdenek Frankenberger, to whom great credit goes for the achievement of this important milestone. Once again, about seven professors and their junior entourage arrived in Bratislava to establish the Department of Basic Sciences. Some professors chose a hybrid solution: while residing in Prague, they commuted to deliver lectures, thus supplementing their income. This kind of "double-dipping" was looked upon with suspicion.[17]

By and large the Czech professors maintained high professional standards, inculcating a humanistic and Hippocratic philosophy which fell upon the fertile soil of their Slovak disciples. These young men mostly came from humble backgrounds from the mountains, valleys and small towns. They created the fount of new graduates in medicine from the late 1920's on. These young enthusiastic mavens-to-be gained entry into all the departments of both clinical disciplines and the basic sciences. They picked up the gauntlet of academic competition in every field, challenging their Czech peers—their work was second to none. But climbing the academic ladder was made extremely difficult for these lads from the lower rungs and, according to the research of Anna Paulinyová, Slovaks were generally promoted more slowly than the Czechs were.[18] The medical doctors graduating from the school and their students rejected the prevailing Czechoslovak philosophy in "their land," and they subscribed to the ideal of home-rule for the Slovak nation. In 1925, one of them, František

Šubík, who was also a promising poet, published a collection of politically-charged poems entitled *On the Guard at Morava* that insinuated the danger of the Czechoslovak policies and their negative economic impact on Slovakia. The government in Prague confiscated the poems in order to avoid a national backlash.[19]

From 1930 on the charge of the young and aspiring Slovak assistant professors was on, and a new generation of teachers, researchers, scholars and clinicians appeared. This created some tensions between the former generation of senior and junior Czechs and the grass roots generation of up-and-coming Slovaks. Unfortunately, the Slovaks split along political lines regarding Czechoslovakism and Slovak nationalism, which demanded autonomy within the Republic. This resulted in a rift that had significant religious underpinnings.

Tensions between the Czechs and Slovaks boiled over during the proceedings for academic advancements of some of the Slovak assistant professors, such as Dr. Gustav Valach and Ladislav Bolcek. Their chances were stymied by the subtle but concentrated efforts of the Czech professors. The most blatant and sinister was the attack of Prof. Dr. Victor Teissler, a physicist, against the academic promotion of a first-rate anatomist, Dr. Július Ledenyi. Ledenyi, who on his father's side was of Hungarian-Catholic extraction, started to study medicine in Budapest in 1922. In 1924 he continued his studies in Bratislava. In Budapest, he was exposed to the teaching of a noted Hungarian anatomist, Dr. Kiss, and later in 1930 he expanded his horizons by studying in universities in Germany, Austria, France and Prague as well. Ledenyi published some of his original observations in respected periodicals.[20]

Despite the recommendations of his professor, Dr. Zdenek Frankenberger, Ledenyi's ally in advancing towards the rank of Lecturer, Dr. Teissler started a malicious campaign against his promotion. Ledenyi was accused of Hungarian irredentism and Teissler, as the Chairman of the fact-finding committee, even asked the Czechoslovak Embassy in Budapest to research his case. Eventually the Ministry of Education in Prague blocked Ledenyi's advancement, even though no evidence of political activities was produced.

This, of course, created a chill between the Slovak medical community as other tensions surfaced between two pediatric starts, Dr. Alois Chura and Dr. Jozef Švejcar. Even after Chura's death in the

1970's, when Švejcar was asked about this outstanding scholar, he could not utter a word of professional appreciation. According to the historian O. V. Johnson, a British diplomat made this succinct observation: "At any celebration or function given by the University of Bratislava, the Czech and Slovak professors do not mix nor do they have any social intercourse."[21] There were ill feelings in the largest department of the Medical School—Internal Medicine—where the Czechoslovaks represented by Dr. L. Dérer were polarized vis-à-vis the Slovak autonomists.

In 1938 still only 30% of the lecturers and professors were Slovaks, and for the entire twenty years of the Republic, all the rectors and deans at the Medical School were Czechs.[22] Historians suggest that the senior Czech professors mostly followed their national and class interests and, instead of recognizing the fallacy of this ideology for the majority of the Slovaks, were agents of Czechoslovakism. Hynek, an outstanding scholar and an honest man, acknowledged that the Czechs indeed had a political goal in disguise which fostered Czechoslovakism in order to educate a new intelligentsia in the Czechoslovak spirit.[23]

Still, these professors maintained high academic standards and professional ethics that were inculcated into the new generation of Slovak academicians. The Czech professors who made a historical contribution to the Medical School in particular were Krystian Hynek, Zdenek Frankenberger, Stanislav Kostlivý, and Jiří Brdlík, outstanding pioneers in their fields. They were instrumental in establishing a Medical Library at the University and a Museum of Human Anthropology. They fostered the inauguration of the Association of Medical Students and founded the medical journal *Bratislavské Lekárske Listy* (The Medical Letters of Bratislava) in 1921 for the communication of advances in medical sciences.[24]

The 1930's brought about increased demands and demonstrations by the students for the upgrading and building of physical plant and dorms for the University and for the introduction of new language laws whereby education would be provided in the language of the land: Slovak. In the Medical School the new generation of Slovak assistant professors asked for greater autonomy in their fields and made remarkable progress despite official foot-dragging policies. Unfortunately, amidst these tensions or because of ideological differences, a dichotomy of minds developed. Some of the Slovak members espoused the Czechoslovak platform of the central government, while the majority raised the flag for a distinct and separate Slovak nationality, claiming their right to Slovak autonomy within the Republic.

In 1931 Professor Hynek left for Prague for the job he coveted. During his tenure as the Chairman of the Department of Internal Medicine in Bratislava, he took a young Slovak assistant professor under his wing, noticing his exceptional talent and interest in hematology, which was one of Hynek's specialties. Hynek, incidentally, was a Catholic and a deeply religious person and the two were drawn together along these lines.

Hynek's protégé, Dr. Emanual Filo (1901–1973), came from a small farmer's family. (Fig. 2.1) Filo was an outstanding student, graduating *magna cum laude* from the Medical School in 1927 at the top of his class. At the graduation ceremony this 6'2" all, handsome man with raven black hair, heavy eyebrows and somewhat sad black eyes, expressed in fluent Latin his deep thanks to his parents for his upbringing and to Rector Hynek for his patronage, and his immeasurable love for his homeland as well. The President of the Republic, T. G. Masaryk, sent a gold wristwatch engraved with the presidential initials, and the University honored Filo with a gold medal, chain and ring. After three years of working under the tutelage of Hynek, Filo was invited to Prague as an Assistant Professor, a position created especially for him as an outstanding Slovak. He remained in Prague for five years and returned to Bratislava as a Lecturer in Internal Medicine. During these years he specialized mainly in hematology and studied abroad in Zurich, Paris, Frankfurt and Stockholm and developed into an exceptional scholar and researcher in the field. He published about sixty papers during these years; a quarter of them were published in distinguished Western journals. He educated a group of followers who were noteworthy associates, and in harmony with him nationally and spiritually as well. Filo was the designated Crown Prince of his department, following in the footsteps of his teacher and mentor, Professor Dr. Hynek.

In the Department of Internal Medicine, Dr. Ladislav Dérer was Filo's professional rival. He was the younger brother of Dr. Ivan Dérer, a Budapest-trained lawyer and ardent Czechoslovakist, who did not speak very fondly of his Slovak brethren. In the mid-1920's, while serving as Secretary of Education in the central government in Prague, Dr. Ivan Dérer was expected to support the newly created University in Bratislava, but he failed to do so.

Dr. Ladislav Dérer (1897–1960), like Filo, started his medical studies in Prague but graduated in Bratislava in 1924. After his graduation, Dérer initially worked as Assistant Professor of Internal Medicine under the tutelage of Dr. Miloš Netoušek, a Moravian who had distinguished himself as a veteran legionnaire in Siberia and was now Dr. Hynek's deputy. Netoušek was an excellent scholar, teacher and clinician who, in 1931, after Hynek's departure to Prague, was appointed as the Chair of the Department of Internal Medicine which he chaired until 1938.

Dr. Ladislav Dérer grew up under Netoušek's guidance, advanced to the rank of Lecturer in 1930, and was named Associate Professor in 1937. He studied pathology in Berlin for two years, but his overall exposure to Western medicine was slight. He was an astute research and mainly published papers regarding hematology, although he also published in the fields of digestion, the liver, circulation and shock. Dérer observed a periodic behavior in the generation of white blood cells, but was unable to elucidate either its etiology or the meaning and importance of this phenomenon. He made assumptions about periodicity or biorhythm in other organ systems that he then related to the regulatory changes of the brain. Dérer, according to his associate Dr. Mikuláš Ondrejička, took a quantum leap hypothesizing that this was a fundamental display of "living matter." These unproven theories, which in the 1930's were difficult to validate with the available scientific technology, were quoted *ad infinitum* by his pupils without further explanation regarding his ideas.[25]

Here it should be noted that Dérer, with his liberal-leftist political convictions, was an unabashed admirer of Soviet science and its medical system. According to his chroniclers, in 1938 his great wish was fulfilled when he visited the Soviet Union with his leftist soulmate and brilliant physician and colleague, Professor Dr. František Simer.[26] Allegedly, Dérer was moved when he visited the laboratory of I. P. Pavlov, the first Russian scientist to receive the Nobel Prize in 1914. Dérer returned ecstatic from what he experienced in that short sojourn and, according to historians, his faith was bolstered in the strength of the Soviet system. Of course the Soviets and Dérer never revealed that Pavlov was the son of an Orthodox priest and that he received his entire training in experimental medicine in Germany well before the Russian Revolution of 1917. Yet the Soviets presented Pavlov as a vindication of the Marxist-materialist approach to the study of the central nervous system in medical science. Pavlov never subscribed to the Marxist philosophy and political tenets, and was adamantly against the attempts of the Communist Party to take over the Academy of Sciences. He was, of course, untouchable and a tremendous asset for Soviet science, which in many ways vulgarized the results of his research.[27]

Soon after Dérer and Simer returned from the Soviet Union, the Munich political crisis affected the Republic and in October 1938 the autonomy of Slovakia proper was declared, thus fulfilling to the letter the Pittsburgh Agreement of 1918.[28] As a consequence, the autonomous government of Slovakia within the truncated Czecho-Slovakia achieved a mutual agreement with the Prague Central Government according to which the contracts of the majority of Czech professors at the University would not be renewed.[29] Retracing the chronicle of thirty-three Czech professors gives some kind of overview of this contentious issue. Out of the thirty-three, six returned to Prague well before this accord (18%). Two had retired earlier and two had died (altogether 12%). Ten professors were declared indispensable by their Slovak colleagues and the Medical School, but two had to be dismissed after one semester (8=24%). Out of the remaining fifteen professors, four were urged to retire based on illness and advanced age of an average of 68 years (12%). The remaining eleven, that is one third, were dismissed in the fall of 1938. It should be added that most of the assistant professors remained in Bratislava and were saved from losing their jobs, and even more importantly, their livelihood after the Universities in Bohemia and Moravia were closed down by the occupying Germans.

These were tumultuous and difficult times for all members of the Medical School, Czechs and Slovaks alike. Loopholes, excuses, reasons and compromises were forged to salvage some appointments but were ineffective for others. Yet there was not an insignificant element of resentment against some of the Czech professors. When Dr. František Šubík, the pathologist, asked his superior Dr. Ján Lukeš to remain, with arrangements being made for him, he brusquely retorted,

"I will not lecture in Slovak under any condition!" There were protestations amongst the faculty members against this political interference, best demonstrated by the lecturer Dr. L. Dérer, who as a leading member of the group of the Czechoslovak persuasion, broke his contract and left the Department of Internal Medicine of the Medical School. Marxist historians labeled his step as protest against the "clerofascist regime"—a sinister coinage indeed—even though the Slovak Government, achieving its autonomy, was still a consenting partner within the rump Czecho-Slovak Republic while Hitler's army stood at the border of the country.[30]

Dérer himself did not fare badly after he left the Medical School. He was appointed as the Chairman of the Department of Internal Medicine of the newest and most modern hospital in the city. This hospital, privately owned by the largest insurance company covering 55,000 blue-collar workers, gave Dérer the freedom to choose his associates from amongst a group of physicians of his own political persuasion, many with significant leftist or crypto-Communist leanings—and this happened under a political regime for which he had no sympathy.[31]

During the war years (1939–45) Dérer was still able to pursue a significant private practice on Poštová Street, bolstering his income.[32] More importantly he kept his finger on the pulse of events at the Medical School by regularly attending the monthly meetings of the faculty, even taking the minutes of the meetings as his signature testifies. He thus had very good insight into the inner sanctum of the Medical School during the war years, being considered a respected colleague or the well-planted mole for the opposition. Dérer correctly sensed that the German juggernaut would run out of steam and be defeated. As a consequence, the Slovak Republic under German protection would disintegrate and the prewar Czechoslovak Republic would reemerge.

The international European theater would develop a new division and new polarity of international forces, whereby the Soviet Union would play a decisive role in this geographic area. Therefore, Dérer started to assiduously learn the Russian language and do his homework for the foreseeable future both in order to be able to communicate with the liberators and to grasp the Russian medical articles from that Soviet science which he so greatly admired.[33] At the same time, as department head, Dérer, an accomplished teacher in his profession, taught his pupils to see the patient in "dialectic unity" with the environment, family, and friends—this more a political slogan than medical science.[34]

At the Medical School the new generation of Slovak professors took over the chairs of the departments and demonstrated their professorial aptitude, proving the fulfillment of their mandate for the school and the Slovak nation. During the Slovak Republic all lectures were presented in the language of the land, even by remaining Czech professors. The name of the University was changed to the unpretentious Slovak University of Bratislava, while for some communications the historical label of "Istropolitana" was resurrected. More importantly, in the insignia of the University, the heads of Saint Cyril and Saint Methodius were introduced—an allusion to a Christian Catholic heritage that reflected the cultural imprint of the nation.

The new faculty members started with great enthusiasm, faith in themselves, optimism and dedication to continue the exemplary professional deliberations of their predecessors, keeping high the banner of excellence despite the ominous political circumstances. Eventually, the political controversy around the appointment of J. A. Ledenyi as Chairman of the Department of Anatomy petered out. He was an outstanding researcher who published prolifically in his field, searching for new answers regarding the origins of congenital anomalies of the heart, lungs, liver and circulatory system. His interests expanded to include the comparative anatomy of other mammals such as cats. Together with the surgeon Dr. S. Kostlivý, he studied the significance of intra-abdominal pressures. An anatomic terminology known as "Nomina Anatomica" in Slovak was published in cooperation with Slovak linguists. Ledenyi's most important work was his *Topographic Anatomy and Dissection*, published in three volumes. His untimely death in 1943 from typhoid fever curtailed the completion of his *Textbook of Anatomy*. It was a tragic and unexpected loss. However, he educated a new generation of anatomists, his successors, Dr. Eugenia Steklačová and Dr. Ernest R. Meitner.

In the field of Basic Sciences, a star was born in Medical Physics in Dr. Jozef Skotnický (b. 1910). Before his graduation from high school he won three state awards in Czechoslovakia in the field of mathematics and his papers were published in the *Review for*

Mathematics and Physics, a distinguished achievement for a Slovak student. After he graduated from the Medical School in 1935, Skotnický immersed himself in medical physics and even tackled problems regarding the basic laws of experimental physics such as the Gaussian theorem of linear equations. His brilliant mind addressed the thermodynamic reaction of metals, important for transistors and computers as well as basic thermodynamic laws and their implications. In medical physics he published works on the effects of electrophysiology on the electrical conduction of nervous fibers and the organization of protoplasma. His publications were known and referred to by professors at Rockefeller University in New York. This extraordinary scientist published over 70 papers, one third of them in Western journals such as the distinguished *Pflugers Archives*, among others.[35]

Dean E. Filo tried to bring Slovak intellectuals home from Prague and abroad. He struck gold when he brought back from Paris Dr. František Valentín, a towering figure in chemistry. Valentín came home to build and buttress the Slovak University and also to lay the foundations for the University of Natural Sciences. Interestingly, he first studied theology in Vienna, as did about one-fourth of the members of the growing Slovak medical fraternity. He was ordained and served as a parish chaplain for two years. Valentín then changed his mind, was suspended by the Vatican, and went on to study chemistry at the noted Czech Technical University in Prague. He was the darling of his Czech professor and patron, Dr. Emil Votoček, with whom he maintained a lifelong friendship. Receiving his Ph.D. in 1930 and a Doctorate in Chemistry in 1937, he worked in Paris at the Sorbonne for two years, doing research in the field of industrial sugars, where he achieved a synthesis of a new sugar (anhydromannosis). In further research he devoted his time to the synthesis of vitamin C. Part of his work was done in conjunction with the Institute de Biologie-Physico-Chimique under the stewardship of Dr. Frederic Jolliot-Curie and at the Institute of Louis Pasteur. Valentín published prolifically in his field.[36] He was a great man and scholar as well as being a superb teacher. Passing his exams was not an easy task. He brought the Department of Medical Chemistry to exemplary heights and a new cohort of talented pupils grew up around him.

The Department of Pathology was led by another erstwhile theology student who first aimed at healing the soul but ultimately ended healing with the body with medicine. Dr. František Šubík (1903–1982) graduated in 1931 from the Medical School and as a young assistant professor threw himself into the field of pathology. In his first years he published about a dozen papers primarily relating to his field.[37] Šubík was known as a very kind man in the true humanist tradition, keen to be help to his fellow human beings, and as an excellent teacher who spent a lot of time with the students. He was a sensitive romantic and a great patriot as well as a noted national poet. The acclaimed Protestant Slovak poet Martin Rázus admired his poetry that expressed his great love for his homeland. Šubík was awarded a prize for literature by the Slovak State and received the Silver medal of the Polish Academy for Literature for his translations of Polish poetry. He was cofounder of a new medical journal, *The Slovak Physician*.

In pharmacology, a new expert was born in the figure of Dr. František Švec (1906–1976), who graduated in 1930 from the Medical School and spent his first three years at the Department of Physiology. Afterwards he joined the Department of Pharmacology where he plunged into the research of this dynamic field and its many puzzles. He devoted himself mainly to cardiac glycosides resulting in a two-volume text which was later translated into Russian. Švec was able to study abroad in Oxford, Vienna, Munich and Basel. An exciting lecturer, he often received invitations to lecture abroad as well. A prolific writer and researcher, he published over one hundred papers, many of them in Western journals. Švec was an amusing and accomplished teacher, very much loved and respected by the medical students. In the late 1950s he was a member of the Committee of the Swedish Academy for the Nobel Prize.[38]

Dr. Vojtech Mucha (1902–1984), a 1929 graduate of Charles IV University in Prague, succeeded the controversial Czech professor Dr. Stanislav Ružicka after he retired. He held the post of Assistant Professor in pathology until 1939. During this period he argued with his Czech boss, Dr. J. Lukeš, who had a condescending attitude vis-à-vis the Slovaks. Once, when a Czech orderly retired from the department and a Slovak was suggested to take his place, Lukeš remarked ironically that a Slovak would not be capable! Mucha, who was present, hit the table and retorted in anger, "Professor, you should not allow yourself such derogatory remarks." In 1939 Much was appointed as head

of the Department of Medical Hygiene, his precipitous career resulting in a professorship in 1943. He published extensively in the field of
environmental hygiene and hydromicrobiology, studying the pollution
of the river Danube, as well as limnology, the microbiology of fresh
water resources.

   In the clinical disciplines, the first Slovak professor who broke
through the Czech ranks was Dr. Michal Seliga (1881–1945). He
studied medicine in Budapest and Kolozsvár (Hungary) and graduated
in 1910. Seliga also started out in a seminary and then switched to
medicine. In 1931 he was already a full professor, one of the first.

   Newborn babies and the dynamic field of pediatrics turned out to
be the great love of Dr. Alois Chura (1899–1979), who became an in-
ternational authority in this field.[39] As was true of most of his fellow
Slovak colleagues, he had humble roots. After high school, during the
First World War, he was drafted into the drills of the Hungarian
"Honvéds" (infantrymen). After the war he attended medical school in
Budapest and graduate in Bratislava in 1923. Chura started to publish
early on, while still in medical school, and the Czech Academy of
Science published one of his papers as its first Slovak publication. He
spent six months in London at the Hospital for Sick Children, and
attended Kings College under the patronage of Dr. R. J. Macdowall.
Studies in Amsterdam, Leiden and Berlin had a lasting impact on this
impressive figure in pediatrics. In 1929, with his monumental work on
childhood diphtheria, he advanced to the post of Lecturer. By 1933 he
was an Associate Professor and in 1936 was nominated a Full
Professor by none other than the president of Czechoslovakia, T. G.
Masaryk. Professor Dr. J. Brdlík was his proud tutor and lifelong
friend. Chura introduced the quantitative evaluation and longitudinal
follow-up in pediatrics, a novelty in his field. In these early years, he
was one of the first to sense the importance of heredity. In his socio-
logical study, a two-volume text entitled *Slovakia Bereft of Youth*, he
and his associates examined over 100,000 infants and children. Based
on this massive work, as well as on his other text, *Pediatric Sociology*,
he lay down the fundamentals for comprehensive care from the prenatal period to late adolescence. While only in his thirties, he had
already established prenatal clinics and clinics for juvenile diabetes,
heart disease and speech disorders. Care for infants with congenital
syphilis was undertaken and courses for midwives and milk kitchens

were founded as well. In this regard he was diametrically opposed to his Czech rival, Dr. Josef Švejcar who started a successful campaign proclaiming processed cow's milk as equivalent to mother's milk. Chura was of the conviction that species-specific mother's milk and nursing were superior, and ultimately his conviction was vindicated. He also successfully attacked the problems of infant mortality and was first in introducing vitamin D orally for the prevention of rickets.[40]

In 1931, Professor Brdlík, together with Dr. Švejcar, returned to Prague and Chura inherited his chair. He published extensively—over 50 articles on genetics, anthropometric research, and the autonomic nervous system. In a second bout of scientific endeavor, he published a monumental text entitled *Respiratory Problems in Children*, which was even translated by the Russians, void of a copyright. Chura was an invited member of many associations such as the German Society for Metabolism, and later a member of the European Branch of the World Health Organization (WHO), as well as a member of the Pediatric Society of Czechoslovakia. As a person he was at first glance a distant, even gruff man, but under his thin crust he was a warm family man with great compassion for the parents of his patients, always being ready to help them. He was a demanding but fair teacher and educated a whole school of pediatricians for his homeland. Chura was a great patriot devoted to his nation, church, and land.

Dr. Karol Matulay (b. 1906) was appointed in 1939 as both a Lecturer in Neurology and Psychiatry and as the Chair of the Department. During his medical studies he was active in the Association of Slovak Students, a group which tried to achieve a better balance between the duties and responsibilities which lay between the Czech founding fathers and the new generation of Slovak academicians. He was a mercurial, bright and inventive man with an inquisitive mind. Barely four years after his graduation from the Medical School in 1934, he pioneered the angiographic diagnosis of brain tumors, a field in whose diagnosis he excelled. Only in Portugal had similar attempts been initiated by Dr. Egas Moniz.[41] In the first ten years of his scientific endeavors he published about thirty papers on brain and spinal tumors, epilepsy and electroshock, later turning his attention to mental retardation and Down's Syndrome in children.

The Department of Dermatology had a rocky start in 1920 when the appointed head, Dr. Antonín Tryb from Prague, failed to show up.

Two years later Dr. V. Reinsberg arrived and developed a solid department, followed by the excellent Dr. J. Treger who took over the Chair after Reinsberg's unexpected and untimely demise. Dr. Treger developed his school of students for the entire country in the following years and served as a dean in 1944.[42]

In the surgical disciplines, Dr. Konštantín Čársky (1899–1987) carried the day after succeeding his father-in-law, the founder of the Slovak surgical disciplines, a Czech from Vienna, Dr. Stanislav Kostlivý. Čársky, who started as a young seminarian in order to fulfill his mother's wishes, graduated from high school in 1917 and was spirited away to remote Albania as a young soldier. After the Great War he matriculated from Charles IV University but graduate from the Medical School in Bratislava in 1924. Šársky, a real surgical talent, followed in the footsteps of his illustrious teacher and rapidly rose up the ranks. In 1939 he was granted a full professorship and became Chairman of the Department. He was one of the very few who, in the early 1930's, at his own expense, visited the United States and such prominent institutions as P. Bent-Bingham Hospital in Boston headed by Dr. H. Cushing, Dr. Crile at the Cleveland Clinic, as well as the Mayo Clinic. This visit was a tremendous professional boost and experience and enabled him to publish over one hundred scientific papers.[43]

Dentistry was covered by a rare local, Dr. Ján Fridrichovský (1896–1978), who quickly advanced in this field. After studies in Bonn, he went on to publish extensively and to educate a large student body.[44]

In the group of Czechs who remained in Slovakia after October 1938, eight were full professors and ten were junior assistant professors. Among these the most prominent were Dr. Jozef Babor, Dr. Anton Gala, Dr. Stanislav Kostlivý and Dr. Jaroslav Sumbal. They retained their Czech identity undisturbed and developed a positive and constructive engagement with the homegrown junior Slovak academicians. They even grew to have an appreciation and love for the people of this land.

The last of these Czech professors, Dr. Hermann Krsek (1897-1983), whose skin and academic career were saved from the fate of the professors in Bohemia when Charles IV University was closed by the Germans, turned out to be a sheep in wolf's clothing. Born in northern Bohemia in what was then called the Sudetenland, his first name was a very German "Hermann." Krsek came from the Medical School of Prague to support the Czech elements in Bratislava from which he had graduated in 1925. He turned out to be an illustrious professor in forensic medicine and was appointed Chair of the Department in 1939. During these years he associated with his philosophical and political brethren, Dr. L. Dérer and Dr. F. Simer. In this year a contractual arrangement with the Medical School created a loophole and Krsek was declared to be indispensable. He pursued his career in Bratislava during the Second World War and even advanced to the rank of Associate Professor in 1940. As we will see, he kept some surprises up his sleeve for his colleagues who had watched out for him and his family.[45]

In the spring of 1939 Hitler decided to liquidate the rump state of Czecho-Slovakia, engulfing Bohemia and Moravia into the German Reich. Under this military pressure there were neither safe harbors nor easy solutions and the Slovaks had to save their small nation. Out of necessity, the interwar Slovak Republic was established but a mere six months later the Second World War had begun. The Western Allies were unable to contain the German "*Drang nach Osten*" with its appetite for more *Lebensraum* and all its unforeseeable consequences for Europe and the entire world.

At this precarious historic time, the goals of the new leadership of the Medical School and the University were to maintain and secure the independence of the University and its academic standards, as well as to save the Medical School from the anti-Christian influence of the ideology of German National Socialism. In the Christian spirit, the fall semester was initiated in 1939 with a festive mass and a hymn, "*Veni sancte spiritus*," which demonstrated the sum and substance of the Catholic majority of the land.

Fortunately, the governance of the University did not slip into the political hands of the new regime. It was left in control of the elected professors and faculty members, even though key positions were ceded to supporters of the Slovak People's Party or their members. As Owen V. Johnson emphasized, many of the professors rejected the tenets of the political platform with its religious underpinnings and some less democratic elements which reflected the tangled political times. The Union of Slovak Professors set a good example by keeping the SPP political manifesto at arms-length, while not hesitating to invite its support when pursuing the school's needs for progress.[46]

In the first days of independence when the dream of many, if not the majority, came through—that is, for the first time in millennia to have their own Slovak Republic—some young professors like Filo, Chura and Šubík dressed up in the uniform of the Slovak People's Party. This was a display of their patriotism, nationalism and love for their homeland, but it was also a sign of the political immaturity and naivete, which would be misunderstood, misinterpreted and construed as evidence of their sympathies for their German "protectors."

Despite these stormy political times, it was obvious that the University and the Medical School could not live in a vacuum and the institution had to fulfill its obligations for higher education: teaching, research and health care for the nation. The Secretaries of Education and Health were rather broadminded, and granted significant latitude vis-à-vis the goals and standards of the professors in producing a new generation of Slovak professionals and in advancing and pursuing their teaching and research. Accordingly, there was an upsurge in enrollment in all departments of the University. There was a 28% increase in the number of graduates during the years 1938 to 1944, mainly in Medicine and Philosophy. Most importantly, according to O. V. Johnson, during the Slovak Republic the government made substantial investments in the University's physical plant and facilities. It also increased the number of Slovak professors and the administrators, speeding up and fostering a Slovak university governance, self-administration and management.[47]

The Deans of the Medical School in the years 1938–1945 were Drs. Chura, Filo, Čársky, Fridrichovský and Treger. Their paramount goal, besides the obvious task of teaching and research, was to safeguard the autonomy of the Medical School in the Slovak cultural traditions and shield it from the influence of German National Socialism and from the opprobrium of A. Rosenfeld's *Rassenhygiene*. Dr. F. Valentín emphatically declared: "We will use the word race only at a horse race!"[48] By and large, the Germanic philosophy was a foreign, unaccustomed intrusion into the Slovak social and cultural life. The Slovaks were seldom exposed the German way of thinking in comparison to the neighboring Czechs who went through history under this influence. Fascism was a foreign ideology for the Slovaks and very few believed in it. A humanistic medicine was incompatible with the German racial and rogue philosophy. Even though the faculty had professional exchanges with Switzerland, Spain, Italy and Hungary, all of them shied away from visits to the Reich and declined lecture invitations, even while some of them were unavoidable.

During the war not a few of the professors at the Medical School, including Drs. Filo and Chura, remained in touch with their Czech colleagues. In fact, Chura, as Dean of the Medical School, accepted a number of Czech students to his school, on the request of Professor Dr. Teyschl from the Medical School of Brno (Moravia), when the Czech universities were shut down.

Dr. Filo, as editor-in-chief of *Medical Letters of Bratislava*, paid major homage in the journal both to his teacher Dr. Ch. Hynek on his 69th birthday in 1939 and to his patron from Prague, Professor Dr. Pelnař in 1942 on his 70th birthday. Filo also shielded the Czech professors Drs. Sumbal, Krsek and Kostlivý, who stayed at the Medical School. Filo returned Kostlivý's notice of dismissal issued by the Ministry of Education, which permitted Kostlivý to stay on. Filo and Chura, opposed to abortions and believing in protecting the sanctity of motherhood, blocked the bills of the German population laws. At this time Dr. Filo was awarded a stipend from the Rockefeller Institute of New York, which he was unable to accept because of the precarious times. Interestingly, in 1940 when the Hitler-Stalin Non-aggression Pact kept German aggression at bay, Filo, as Dean of the Medical School, was invited to celebrate the 125th anniversary of the foundation of the Lomonosov University in Moscow. He traveled with his entourage to Berlin where he was welcomed at the Soviet Embassy by its ambassador, Skvarcev. The delegation flew to Moscow where, during the celebration, Filo was presented an award "*Za peredovaju nauku*," for his advancements in science. During this meeting in Moscow he met Dr. Zděnek Nejedlý, the Czech Communist ideologue who was in exile. Filo also met with Rector Butjagin and A. Y. Vychinsky, the future prosecutors of the infamous Stalin trials. The Slovak Minister of Health, Dr. J. Sivák, was received by the Soviet Secretary of State, V. O. Molotov. The Slovak delegation visited the Medical School in Leningrad, where Filo was surprised by an exhibition of his scientific papers that had been published abroad. He was bestowed the greatest honor on May 1, 1940, when he and his group were seated on the top of Lenin's Mausoleum in a red box in order to watch the largest military parade of the year. He later learned that he was followed throughout the entire visit by the Gestapo and was later questioned about why he had avoided visiting the German Ambassador to Moscow.

Filo was a man of the highest moral standing and he never hid the fact that he was devout Catholic. This did not sit well with the Germans, who objected to him as Dean, and later Rector, of the University. He was a follower of the Christian path, ergo he had principled objections to the Nazi ideology. The Germans tried to infiltrate the Department of Internal Medicine and the Department of Surgery under the chairmanship of Dr. K. Čársky with German physicians, but both Filo and Čársky resisted and furthermore offered their resignations. Eventually, Filo was forced to resign as Rector when he blocked the appointment of a physician who was a protégé of Heinrich Himmler, the Nazi Police Chief. Filo also avoided lecturing in the Reich after being warned by the Slovak Secret Service that he could jeopardize his life.

In the years 1942–42, Filo, as Rector of the University, harbored around 700 students from different schools in Bulgaria who had been expelled by the Czech Protectorate. The Bulgarian King Boris II personally awarded Filo a medal for his actions and an icon of St. Clement, who was a student of Sts. Cyril and Methodius.

On the home front, Filo was instrumental in the academic advancement of his associates, Drs. G. Bárdos, M. Sivák, G. Onrejička, S. Sitáj, K. Holomán, F. Dragula, and also the talented Dr. J. Žucha whom he brought home from Prague.

As the Second World War dragged on in the winter of 1943, and in particular after the Battle of Stalingrad, conditions in Slovakia started to deteriorate. The deportations of Jews hit the medical community very hard. According to government statistics, in 1938 the Jewish population made up about 4% of the nation, but in the medical field over 40% of the doctors were of Jewish background.[49] Filo shielded Jewish students by listing them under aliases. With the great help of Dr. F. Šubík, who was in charge of the Department of Health, they placed many Jewish doctors in small remote hospitals, small spas and sanatoriums in the mountains of Slovakia, saving them from deportation—Drs. Deutch, Weiner, Weiss and Wunch, as well as Drs.

Demant, Guensberger, Hegyi and Kunstadt, to name only a few. Šubík intervened in Berlin through diplomatic connections on behalf of a deported respected colleague, Professor Dr. F. Simer, but to no avail. To the great loss of the Medical School and humankind, Simer perished at the hands of the Gestapo.

The last challenge for these faculty members came during the Slovak National Uprising in August of 1944, which broke out in the heartland of Slovakia. Many students, junior physicians and assistant professors of the Medical School joined the groundswell of opposition against the German oppressors and their collaborators, offering their help and services in health care but ultimately serving as student guards in maintaining public order. At one of these political rallies, which supported the reestablishment of the former Czecho-Slovakia and pledged allegiance to the Soviet Union and the ideology of Marxism and Leninism, a young lecturer, Dr. Karol Rebro, boosted their morale with an ideological pep talk. This man resurfaced soon in Bratislava, crossing the lives of many professors of the Medical School as their arbitrator. The uprising collapsed in two months time and the medical students, now in their early twenties, poured back to the winter semester and the Medical School seeking its cover and protection. Needless to say, a majority of these students, most of them of Protestant background, were not only against the Germans and their lackeys but also for the restoration of the old Czechoslovak Republic. Likewise, the young assistant professors came back from their extended vacations, so to speak. But now, under German pressure in Bratislava, new officials were installed in the Ministry of Education who, at the explicit demand of the Germans, tried to encroach on the remaining autonomy of the University.

Again Filo, together with the other faculty members, and especially Šubík, saved many students, especially the group of Communists students and their ringleader, J. Krivoš, from the county of Liptov. All the junior faculty members—Drs. Kindernay, Blaškovič, Hensel and others—returned to their departments unharmed. Needless to say, all the department heads were in tremendous danger and under surveillance of the Gestapo. Dr. Filo and the others were constantly spied upon. Towards the end of the war, Dr. Filo endangered his life by hospitalizing—that is to say *hiding*—a Communist bigwig and member of the underground Slovak National Council, F. Kubáč, within the Department of Infectious Diseases, where he remained quarantined. In other departments the chairmen were well aware of the political persuasions of many leftist doctors like Dr. J. Michaličková in Pediatrics, but they turned a blind eye towards them. When Himmler sent another German doctor to snoop around, Filo, as Rector, resigned in protest of this breach. Later Dr. Valentín followed suit and relinquished his duties as Rector when he was forced to carry out orders against his personal beliefs and convictions.

As the war was inching toward a conclusion, the Germans, in a last ditch effort, wanted to appropriate all technical equipment and instruments of the medical institutions. The professors, on the other hand, wanted to salvage everything for their school and nation. (Fig. 2.2) They were able to thwart these German efforts in the final days of confusion and chaos with the help of some patriotic government officials. Instead of being exported to Germany, the machines, under cover of darkness, were smuggled east to the middle of Slovakia. Here, in small spas and clinics, the equipment was placed underground, hidden under roofs, or cemented into hidden pockets in the walls.

This tumultuous era came to a finish at the end of April 1945 when Slovakia was "liberated" by the Red Army. The nation was flooded by Soviet secret agents. The entire underground movement of partisans and Communist fighters who fought the Germans and their Slovak collaborators surfaced and a fundamental overhaul and political regrouping began at this seminal "change of the guard," which transformed the land for half a century. Now old political scores were due to be settled and the political stage was set with the hammer and sickle prepared for the showdown.

Fig. 2.1: Dr. Emmanuel Filo

Fig. 2.2: Members of the Faculty at the Medical School, 1944

3
Under the Red Flag –
or Homo Homini Lupus

Barely did the guns fall silent on May 9, 1945, the day of victory, when the old Czechoslovak actors surfaced, together with the younger generation of new leftist radicals. The Soviet Army juggernaut, meanwhile, rounded up the members of the previous political regime. Since the fall of 1944, just before the war ended, the underground Slovak National Council was already in place to run the country when the time came. All of its members were for the restoration of the previous Czechoslovak Republic as representative of the Czechoslovak philosophy. The Council was composed of mostly Protestant politicians and anti-church elements with the powerful participation of the Slovak Communists, who enjoyed and were bolstered by the presence of the Soviet Army and its agents. The dawn of a new era appeared under a new protector—the Soviet Union.

It was obvious that the first homegrown, mostly Catholic, Slovak intellectual elite at the University would be severely punished because of their different political views and convictions, and because they had dared to dream of their own Slovak nation-state 50 years ahead of its time. A political witch-hunt with significant religious overtones erupted at the Medical School and at the University right after the Red Army liberated Bratislava in April of 1945. With the goal of the restoration of the prewar Czechoslovak order, the rush to judge and the speed of political reprisals were astounding. A grand regrouping within the Slovak intelligentsia began.

None of the faculty members broke the law or perpetrated any criminal, civic or political transgression during the Second World War. The mere fact that these professors served as elected deans and professors, a great honor and distinction indeed, was regarded as evidence that they were willing agents of the interwar Slovak regime.

That was a misinterpretation and tremendous leap in the face of reality. During the war they regarded their whole professional life as a service to their nation, even under the dire circumstances, and they could not fathom professional exile when they, as scholars, teachers and researchers, were most needed.

The frontal attack on these university professors was led by the Minister of Education, Ladislav Novomeský (1904–1974), a Communist poet and writer, and his spiritual acolyte in faith, Dr. L. Dérer, who was immediately appointed (not elected) as the Dean and Commissioner Plenipotentiary at the Medical School.

Novomeský was an interesting but highly controversial figure. An emotional lyricist and Slovak nationalist, he was at the same time a devout and unconditional Communist Party disciple. Born in Budapest before the First World War (his father was a tailor), he came from a religious Lutheran family. He failed to fulfill his mother's desire to become a Protestant minister. Instead, amidst the squalor of the First World War and the Bolshevik revolution of the Jewish-Hungarian POW Béla Kun, he was smitten by the Red revolution. He remarked, "Even today, I chant the Internationale with the lyrics which I learned then!" During the revolution he acquired the ruby-red brand from which he never wavered.[1]

After 1919 Novomeský's family returned to Slovakia and in 1923 he graduated from Teachers College. In 1925 he joined the Communist Party as a prolific journalist while working in the mining district of northern Moravia and soon published his first collection of poems under the title, *The Sabbath*. Novomeský rose to prominence in Prague as an editor of the Communist daily *Rudé Právo* (Red Light) and its Marxist ideologue. He was jailed repeatedly by the government. When Bohemia and Moravia were seized by Hitler in 1939, Novomeský returned to Bratislava and, with the help of his friends, was employed by the economic press. During the Slovak Republic he remained low-key, under surveillance but unharmed. His regular meetings in the Café Metropol with the Communist avant-garde, his friend Dr. Gustáv Husák and others were a display of "normalcy and tolerance" during the Second World War. In 1943 he joined the resistance and was a member of the then illegal Slovak National Council, participating in the Slovak National Uprising in August 1944. In October 1944, hidden in the bomb bay of a fighter, he flew to London for an encounter and dressing down by the exiled President Eduard Beneš, who dismissed Slovak aspirations for national equality in the postwar Czecho-Slovakia. In January 1945, he returned victoriously from Moscow to Czechoslovakia with the Red Army.[2]

After the war, as the Minister of Education, he had the upper hand and followed the line of the unimpeded cleansing of "traitors and collaborators" in the schools of the land, especially at the University. He was aware of the political sympathies within the body of Slovak university professors, the so-called Slovak autonomists. Novomeský and his cronies knew whom to label as such, whom to sacrifice, and whom to spare for a while only to eliminate later. Allegations were considered the same as proof of physical evidence of collaborations during these days of settling old political accounts and in creating professorial positions for themselves. The law of the land and academia was subordinated to hard-core politics. During the Slovak Republic the University was under certain political constraints but its autonomy was by and large respected. Now the game had changed. The University had to give up its autonomy when the new actors were willing to subjugate it to the new political order, headed by the Communists, who completely dominated the field after 1948.

To create the semblance of fair hearings or fact-finding bodies, certifying commissions were established at the University and within its schools to perform background checks on the activities of the professors during the interwar Slovak Republic. At the Medical School, the chairman of the commission was Dr. L. Dérer. To give an appearance of due process to these proceedings, a professor from the School of Law, Dr. K. Rebro, was made co-chairman. He was a graduate of Law in 1936 and during the Slovak Republic advanced to the rank of Lecturer and Associate Professor, even though he was known for his left-wing orientation. Rebro was an active participant in the Slovak National Uprising and an ideologue of it. In 1945 after the Red Army's liberation of the land, he became a "legal expert" at the Ministry of the Interior.

The certifying commission at the Medical School—indeed, a revolutionary tribunal—was composed of professors Sumbal, Koch, and Krsek, all of "Czechoslovak" persuasion and the known partisans Dr. Thurzo and Dr. Barbarič. Dr. V. Haviar, who had saved two Communist ringleaders—Široký and David—when they escaped from prison by transferring them clandestinely to his private car to join the advancing Red Army, joined the commission as well. The only Catholic in this group was Professor J. Červenanský, whose political credentials for this task were bolstered by both his wife, who was a of Czech extraction, an otherwise illustrious historian, and his father-in-law, Dr. Stuchlík, a prominent psychiatrist, who made his career and fortune in the eastern Slovak city of Košice. He was also an enthusiastic admirer of Soviet science and had visited the Soviet Union. This commission worked hand-in-hand with the Minister of Education and comrade in arms, Dr. Ondrej Pavlík, a Communist zealot and Party apparatchik who even emulated his ideological idol Lenin by growing a goatee. The Ministry of Health, headed by Dr. Ján Ševčík and later Dr. William Thurzo, acted as an executive arm, while Dr. L. Dérer had unrestricted power. The process of hearings and arbitration was secret, but word leaked out that it was not without some shouted repartee. According to an unconfirmed source, no minutes of the proceedings were officially taken. The only professor lucky enough to be spared this vicious charade was Dr. M. Šeliga, who died in March 1945.

The first group to be disposed of were professors Filo, Chura, Šubík and Skotnický. Dr. Filo was dismissed immediately on April 30, 1945, even before the war had ended, with the document of discharge issued on October 18, 1945. All four of them had to retroactively vacate their posts and departments and their salaries were halted. The reasons given were that they were all members of the Slovak People's Party and had contacts with leaders of this party and were thus inevitably representatives of the former regime.

But this was only the beginning of the trials Filo would have to face. Before the end of the war, Filo had received offers to take a position as a research hematologist abroad but had declined. He was now transferred to a small district town in the heartland of Slovakia as the Head of a small Department of Internal Medicine, which had been quickly assembled in two ramshackle family villas. When the Secretary of the Slovak Academy wanted to develop a small research laboratory for this illustrious scholar, the attempt was thwarted. In 1947 Filo was accused of illegal activities against the state and his house was searched but nothing was found. As the Communists came to power in 1948, Filo was repeatedly interrogated as a Vatican agent and religious fanatic, ridiculed and chastised by the agents of the police for being a practicing Catholic. All five of his children were expelled from their grammar schools and institutions of higher learning were closed to them.

In 1950, by sheer coincidence, I, as a medical student, met Dr. Filo while on summer internship in his makeshift department. During his rounds he showed us his forte as a sophisticated, extremely knowledgeable teacher. He presented an interesting case to us where a young woman was seriously ill with a severe infection of her heart valve. Besides the huge amounts of antibiotics she received, she was also to consume half a pint of freshly squeezed carrot juice. Why was that, we wondered? To our surprise, Filo seemed to know or presuppose what we preach today—that anti-oxidants such as vitamin A from carrots are beneficial or protective of the endothelium or interior lining of valves and vessels.

In 1953 Filo was arrested when Catholic Church members were rounded up as the only ideological bastion against rampaging Communism. This time he was accused of concealing a priest in his department as just a few years prior he had saved the life of a Communist leader, comrade Kubáč. Filo was charged as an agent against the state and jailed for 18 months in the infamous prison of Pancrác near Prague. While imprisoned he lost 60 pounds, his body became covered with boils and he developed hypertension and consequently congestive heart failure. In 1960 he was dismissed as the head of his small department and worked as a resident physician. This situation lasted ten more years until he was exonerated of all his alleged political transgression, but by then Filo was a broken man.

Likewise, Dr. A. Chura, an outstanding scholar, was dismissed on the same charges as Filo. His dismissal was signed by Dr. L. Dérer. In addition, he was accused of being instrumental in the dismissal of the Czech professors in 1938 and of having had reservations against some Protestant colleagues, even though a group of them—some outright crypto-Communists—who were part of his department, had found safe haven there. His membership on the editorial boards of some German medical journals "proved" his "fascistic" sympathies. No evidence was provided for these charges. Furthermore, Chura was the only tenured professor appointed in 1936 by President T. G. Masaryk himself. As this was a lifelong appointment, the Ministry of

Education had no legal right to dismiss him. In 1947, a search warrant was issued permitting his house to be searched but nothing tangible was found.

After his dismissal from the University, Chura was appointed Head of a tiny Department of Pediatrics in the small town of Stropkov in the eastern-most part of Slovakia on the Russian border. When the newly appointed Communist administration at the hospital learned who was supposed to come, they sent a telegram: "We don't want any dismissed university professors who are enemies of the state!"[3]

Eventually Chura was appointed as Head of the Department of Infectious Diseases and shortly thereafter Head of the Department of Pediatrics in the nearby town of Trenčín. Here, with unbroken professional spirit, and as one of the founders of Slovak pediatrics, he established the Institution for Post-Graduate Education, and led this center of learning to the highest academic standards in the country.

At the certifying proceedings in 1945, the lawyer, Professor K. Rebro, was exceptionally rude to Chura. Ironically, a few years later Rebro's son fell ill and the professors at the Medical School were unable to cure him. Rebro had to step down from his high horse and through an intermediary sent his wife to beg for Chura's help. Chura refused to see Rebro himself but immediately accommodated his wife and the boy was saved. Rebro was not the only leading Communist who sought Chura's help: when Professor Maslow, the Secretary of Health of the Soviet Union, visited Prague in the early 1960s, he requested to meet Dr. Chura, the author of the seminal textbook of respiratory diseases in children. The government in Prague had to scramble to fulfill the wishes of the coveted Soviet guest to meet Dr. Chura.

The Professor of Pathology Dr. Šubík, a humanist and sensitive poet as well, who abhorred any violence, also faced tragedy. Before the Second World War had ended, as the Chief of Health Service, he had helped and protected many Jewish physicians from deportation, hiding them in small remote hospitals. He did this for many doctors and students who had fought the Germans in the Slovak National Uprising in the fall of 1944. Doctors who had been protected by him—among them Drs. D. Blaškovič, J. Petelen and W. Paulinyi-Tóth—testified in his favor before the commissions. According to Dr.

Sumbal, whom he had shielded as well, Šubík had dared to remove Hitler's plaque from the dean's office.

Two years after the Germans attacked the Soviet Union in 1941, mass graves were discovered in Poland which, according to the Germans, were Polish officers and soldiers killed by the Soviet Secret Police on Stalin's orders while laboring in Soviet gulags. The Germans seized this opportunity to gear up their propaganda machine and asked the International Red Cross to send a commission of international experts to investigate the crime. The Germans asked for an expert from Bratislava but declined the proposed forensic pathologist Dr. H. Krsek because of his Czech background. Dr. Šubík was then substituted as the general pathologist.

The group of experts flew via Berlin to Smolensk and traveled by car to the area of the mass graves. About 2,500 corpses were found, out of which 1,500 Polish officers were identified by autopsy. They were mostly reservists, the cream of the Polish intelligentsia. The victims were killed by a single bullet to the nape of the neck and then finished off by Soviet bayonets, leaving a typical asterisk-shaped stab wound, unique to this type of Soviet weapon. Local peasants and railroad men were witnesses and corroborated the findings. The final evidence was presented in a document and signed by all experts under German pressure (Fig. 3.1).

After his return from Poland in May, 1943, Šubík was asked by the Slovak government and the Germans to address the public by radio and present his findings while speaking to a large audience in a lecture hall. Šubík was quite matter-of-fact and confirmed the execution of the Polish officers by the Soviet secret agents and ended his presentation by warning the nation of the face of the spread of Bolshevism, which soon proved to be fatal for him. The Soviets, of course, rejected the findings as German propaganda; it was only in 1990 that the Russians admitted to these atrocities and expressed their apologies to the Polish nation.

In March 1945, together with Slovak government officials, Dr. Šubík left for Austria with his pregnant wife and small son before the arrival of the Red Army. They surrendered to U.S. military forces. In a refugee camp his wife delivered their second son. The U.S. authorities then transferred the entire Slovak entourage to Czechoslovak government agents who transported them to Prague. Šubík, now separated from his family, was concerned that he would be deported to the Soviet Union as others had been. He was eventually tried and sentenced as a collaborator of the previous regime but so many people testified to his decency and assistance to others that he received a jail term of only two and a half years. Even L. Novomeský, his literary and ideological adversary, sent him a message in jail, "Be happy where you are otherwise they [the Soviet Secret Police] will deport you," thus inadvertently giving testimony about the political methods of the times.[4] After Šubík served his jail sentence he remained without a job for over a year, but in 1950 he was employed as a pathologist in a small hospital.

Seeing the relentless witch-hunt of the Communists and the arrests of innocent people in his country, on April 28, 1952, with the help of a Silesian clergyman, Father Révész, Šubík and his family crossed the Morava River in a dinghy to the Austrian side and went into exile. In 1953 he was able to emigrate to the U.S. and found work as a pathologist. In his free time, Šubík returned to his beloved poetry as a bard for his exiled brethren. He also translated the poems of Oscar Wilde and the works of Sophocles and Karol Woytyla, who became Pope John Paul II.

The fourth victim of the certifying proceedings was the brilliant physicist Dr. J. Skotnický. He was immediately dismissed as Head of the Department of Physics. The document was signed by the vicious Communist Dr. Ondrej Pavlík. Skotnický's salary was stopped and he was prevented from lecturing even though a replacement was not found for him. Professor Dr. F. Švec tried to save him but the vindictive Dr. H. Krsek blocked any exemption. The new authorities at the Medical School tried to dig up political dirt to indict Skotnický. They scrambled for gossip and unsubstantiated rumors amongst his associates and even his students. Skotnický was the main target of many failing students who were looking for revenge. Some of them claimed he addressed the students in 1939 by quipping, "I welcome you in your own country set free from Czech vassalage." Recalling Dr. Teissler's anti-Slovak campaign, Skotnický, from his point of view, would have felt justified for this address if he did, in fact, ever uttered this welcome. The students even accused him of undignified behavior when he dressed in a heavier gown during the harsh winter. Some Protestant colleagues claimed that at the time of the Slovak

National Uprising, Skotnický, in a huff, had wished that their stronghold be blown away. Most importantly, he was accused of wanting to evacuate his department's equipment to Germany, which he promptly disproved with available documents regarding these unsubstantiated accusations. On the contrary, he provided proof that he hid the equipment by plastering it into the walls thereby saving it for his department. These allegations by and large were nothing but political sorcery and in a political atmosphere lacking legality nothing could save these men when others were lying in wait for their posts. The best brains of a small nation were disposed of as easily as if they grew on trees.

For the next batch of professors a tug-of-war developed between the different members of the Ministry of Education and the Ministry of Health Care, with conflicting decisions. During a period that lasted about two years, the accused faculty members defended themselves with the help of legal advice and connections. Most of the allegations against the professors went nowhere. Some of the professors were punished or disciplined or even dismissed one day and then a few days later reinstated, depending on who their protector was. But whoever was on Novomeský's enemy list was liquidated. The leading surgeon, Dr. K. Čársky, was demoted and dismissed as the Chairman of the Department because he served as the Dean of the Medical School during the interwar Slovak Republic, but was reinstated after an appeal by Dr. O. Pavlík himself. Likewise, Dr. J. Fridrichowský, a former Dean, was dismissed as the Chairman of the Department of Dentistry, but remained as a lecturer with a lower rank. Objections were made that his roots were of local German background, and eventually he, too, was dismissed. Professor Dr. F. Valentín was dismissed from the faculty of the School of Natural Science, which he had founded, but still remained at the Medical School. His liabilities were that he had displayed a portrait of Msgr. Hlinka in his office and had held lectures in Germany and fascist Romania, thus "proving: his sympathies for these regimes.

There were other contentious "unresolved" cases such as that of Dr. Michal Sivák, Associate Professor and Head of the Department of Ear, Nose and Throat. Minister Novomeský insisted on his removal because of Sivák's alleged Hungarian political sympathies, exemplified by studying in Budapest, the city were Novomeský was born.

Sivák's rapid academic advancement and his alleged antisocial conduct vis-à-vis his patients, which had apparently been witnessed by Dr. V. Haviar, a cardiologist, and Dr. L. Jakubec, an army doctor, also hurt him. One has to wonder how these doctors could have witnessed such a tiff when they were from a different department altogether.

The Neurologist-in-Chief, Dr. K. Matulay, was targeted by Minister Novomeský and, even with the assistance of a lawyer, he lost. A member of the Slovak People's Party and a Slovak activist as a medical student, he allegedly fomented the dissent of the students against the Czecho-Slovak Republic. In 1939, he supposedly thwarted the academic advancement of Dr. J. Černáček, an Assistant Professor from Prague. It was charged that Matulay, as a neurologist, was not using and applying Pavlovian methods in his lectures and practice. The coup de grâce was a claim that in 1941 Matulay and a friend invested some money in small plant of 15 employees, OPTOCHEMA, manufacturing over-the-counter drugs. Unfortunately for him, this business had previously been owned by Dr. Donát, a Jewish physician who, after the war, challenged Matulay's claim. Even though Matulay was legally exonerated of any wrongdoing and his dismissal from the Medical School declared illegal, Novomeský's decision stuck and the dismissal was definitive.

The rest of the faculty was certified at the hearings by the commission but during these hearings brawls developed when Dr. Švec was almost incriminated by Dr. Haviar, an Assistant Professor in Cardiology. Haviar insinuated that Švec had contacts with Croatian fascists. However, evidence was not provided and, as in the majority of cases, only forged concoctions and allegations were hurled against honest people. Dr. Švec warded off these unsubstantiated and venomous accusations but his adversaries did not forget this blemish.

After the dismissals of Filo and others, there was a scramble for their posts. Dr. L. Dérer took Filo's job as Chairman of the Department of Internal Medicine and thus was able to develop a school of his disciples. He remained the most revered physician of the country while Filo's professional work was totally suppressed and even his ghost was purged from the Medical School. Dr. A. Chura's replacement was more difficult since nobody could really fill his shoes. For some years the Department of Pediatrics was led by a lecturer who had been out of academic medicine for years and had run a home for underprivileged children. Eventually, the department was split in two and Chura's division was awarded to his former assistant professor Dr. Jaroslava Michaličková, a Communist.

Fortunately, in the Department of Pathology, Dr. Šubík was replaced by his colleague, the scholarly and colorful Dr. Frank Klein, who returned to the Medical School that he had left in 1936 for "personal reasons." These had most probably been reasons regarding the doubtful political future as a person of Jewish background facing the approach of Fascism. Klein survived the Second World War as a pathologist in a district hospital because he had been shielded by a priest. He was one of the few who had excellent training in his field because of additional studies abroad in Austria and Germany.[5] After the war he returned to Bratislava. To demonstrate his scorn and protest against the previous political regime, he dressed in the German brown shirt uniform without epaulets. Klein, an honest, principled, and very decent man, did not fathom the future surprises in store for him.

In medical physics Dr. Skotnický's place was eventually taken by a radiologist. Coincidentally, a representative of the Rockefeller Institute was looking for Skotnický but it was too late. Dr. Matulay's post was taken by his rival, the Prague-trained Dr. J. Černáček, and the Department of Ear, Nose and Throat was filled by Dr. Ján Lajda, a practitioner in the clinic of a social insurance company. His postdoctoral thesis was the object of significant professional disapproval but because of his political orientation and the lack of other candidates, he got the job.

Interestingly, efforts to re-invite Czech professors from Prague to fill some of the vacant positions were made by Dr. Sumbal, of Czech background, who had worked normally at the Medical School during the Slovak Republic. However, Dérer put his foot down. Even he wanted to keep the Slovak turf at the Medical School for his brethren.

A Communist takeover of the Republic was achieved in February 1948 with far-reaching consequences for the whole University and Medical School. Knives were sharpened and drawn and all hell broke loose when the final showdown and settling of scores began by the Action Committee at the Medical School. The Dean, Professor Dr. Švec, as well as a final group of professors of the old order, all Catholics, were attacked and almost all of them dismissed.

The fundamental political reasons for these latest dismissals were confirmed by a letter of the Chairman of the Czechoslovak Legionnaires, J. Bahurinský, a Communist, dated September 27, 1947. Based on an anonymous informer, the letter claimed a fictitious plot against the state. The letter demanded that the Medical School reexamine and recertify Professor J. Antal, who allegedly wanted to evacuate the equipment of the Department of Physiology to Germany. It claimed that Professor Dr. Švec hosted the Ambassador to Bulgaria, who was purportedly a member of the Gestapo, even though he was not German. It further stated that Professor Dr. Čársky ostensibly pushed Professor Dr. St. Kostlivý, who was his father-in-law, out of the Chairmanship. It also alleged that Professor Dr. Mucha had a negative relationship to the Czechoslovak Republic and was responsible for the "fascistic" methods at the Ministry of Health, as well as touting the old litanies against Drs. Filo, Chura and Matulay, all of whom had already been dismissed.

Another letter of the same date came from the Center of the Slovak Partisans and was signed by General Secretary S. Falťan. Falťan again alluded to a plot against the state among the students at the Medical School and held the professors responsible. The prime target of the letter was once again Dr. Švec because of his sudden ascendancy to the rank of Professor, his membership on the board of the Slovak Pharmaceutical Company and Medica, whose board included German physicians who were labeled Fascists because of their nationality. Objections were made that Švec frequently lectured in German and kept a Slovak flag in his office. Also at a medical conference in 1946 in the Tatras some remarks of Dr. Švec were overheard wherein he praised the working conditions during the interwar Slovak Republic. Dr. F. Valentín's fate was sealed as old charges were repeated against him of making a personal profit from being a board member and expert and many chemical plants. A most preposterous charge was made as well that he did not have a medical degree, therefore he could not be a professor of chemistry at the Medical School. Professor of Urology Dr. J. Jakšy was attacked because of lecturing too frequently abroad, especially in Germany, and for his "business" and financial interests and service fees. Even Professor Dr. J. Tréger of Dermatology, the only Protestant, was attacked for his professional incompetence.

In these two and a half years of political cleansing with its un-mistakable religious undertones, more than 50 percent of tenured pro-fessors were dismissed. The last wave of dismissals sent shock waves through the academic community and student body. The abrupt removal of the Dean was an especially emotional and painful event. Suddenly no one was secure at the Medical School—everyone felt dispensable and fearful of when his own time would come.

A vivid memory of mine amidst these political upheavals was one bright sunny day in early spring of 1948 when we gathered to hear Dr. Valentín deliberate with clarity and listen to his at times amusing presentation in chemistry. A tall, robust man with obviously intelligent black eyes and graying hair, he was an impressive personage indeed. We enjoyed his sparkling performance but he did not inform us that it was his swan song. The next day a man of about 5 feet fall showed up for the lecture in chemistry. Seeing his insecure demeanor and trembling hands, unable to find his place, we though that this was new orderly. His blond hair was parted on the right side and fell into his face that was demarcated by heavy brows and narrow slits for blue eyes. "I am Dr. Ján Kubis," he uttered in a raspy voice, eyes on the ground. "I am your new chemistry professor." The gasp of disbelief that spread through the auditorium full of agitated students was followed by stupefied silence and numbness. We could not under-stand or even hear what he was talking about because of our shock and bewilderment at learning that Valentín, a towering chemist, had been sacked. We learned that this new man was a chemist from an oil refinery who got the job because he was an ardent Communist, his only qualification. He had no experience to present medical chemistry and his lectures were read out of the textbook. They were dull and dreary and his performance was insecure and unconvincing. He never looked anyone in the eye and we were glad when we passed the exam and could forget this poor chap.

Dr. Švec was not allowed to lecture or even finish his ongoing experiments at the Department of Pharmacology and he ended up at the Institute for Oncology, remaining for years the leading figure in his field. A younger associate supplanted his place and later the Chair was awarded to a Communist junior, Dr. Ján Kovalčík. Dr. Jakšy, the urologist, left for Western Europe and ended up in the U.S. after his dismissal.

Comrade Novomeský, who could not even appreciate the medical competence and value of his victims, initiated the political turnover at the Medical School and the dismissal of the best professionals and teachers in their fields. Unfortunately, the people who knew the caliber of scientists the school was losing were also his disciples, Dean and Commissioner Dr. L. Dérer and his friend and successor, the éminence grise, Dr. H. Krsek.

After the victorious Communist putsch, it became more clear that at this time a Czechoslovak persuasion and condemnation of the Slovak state would not be sufficient to move one to the top of the professional ladder—active membership in the Communist Party was required to stay at the helm. The Central Committee of the Communist Party had to give the final approval for any professorship, thus politicizing the academic process and killing any autonomy at the University. Now professors had to address each other as "comrades," no longer as "colleagues," as they had done in the past. The actual election process of faculty members and officials was abolished and replaced by a process of political appointment of the so-called *nomenklatura*, or professors chosen and approved by the Communist Party. The entire organizational structure of the school was overhauled and the faculty had to incorporate into any decision-making process new and self-proclaimed political players who, under the Party aegis, followed their own very personal interests and agendas.

At the Medical School an Action Committee was established (Fig. 3.2) from different departments which was made up of the same Communist professors, mainly junior members of the faculty and students, as well as non-medical members of the Communist Party of the school who had significant proletarian and blue-collar credentials, thus giving birth to a new, illegal shadow government. Its members snooped and investigated the political background of every member of the faculty, especially the senior members who were their main targets due to their presumed bourgeois "old-fashioned" or reactionary views or their insistence on medical science. The ultimate goal was to replace them with the junior Communist avant-garde who would now take charge. This class struggle flourished under the leadership of comrade Milan Praslička, a newly graduated doctor.

The Medical School and each of its departments had its own cell of the Communist Party that was composed of neophyte members. In

1948 membership in the Communist Party grew ten times more than it had in the previous two years. The professors and departmental chairmen's decisions were totally dependent on this anti-professional party where even the cleaning woman had an equal or pivotal voice since she represented the working class. This body was a determining force for political and ideological reeducation or brainwashing, raising a new type of physician who rejected the Hippocratic philosophy and swore allegiance instead to the Party and to class struggle. A siege mentality of hysteria and vigilant suspicion of everyone was the order of the day.

Other important political forces at the Medical School were the Union of all of the Employees (ROH) and, at the student level, the Czechoslovak Youth Organization with its garrulous president, Dušan Bruchač. His first achievement was the dissolution of the historic Medical Students Club, which he folded into his organization that served as the tentacles of the Communist Party. Many of his lieutenants were former partisans who claimed special privileges and leniency in their exams, pressuring professors through this organization to let them pass difficult exams, especially those in anatomy and pathology.

Right after the "Victorious February," Dr. H. Krsek, appointed as the new Dean, followed in the footsteps of his confrere Dr. L. Dérer and joined the Communist Party. From then on, for almost ten ears, he alternated with Dr. L. Dérer in the office of the Dean of Medical School. Krsek was the éminence grise and politically the most powerful member of the faculty, the real Machiavelli and kingmaker. All new appointments and reappointments had to go through him. Krsek, together with the Communist Party and the Ministry of Education, turned out to be a prime mover in the transformation of the Medical School into a new Soviet model. This tripartite force was responsible for and instrumental in the total overhaul of the educational structure of the Medical School.

As the minutes of the faculty meetings—now renamed University Staff Meetings—indicate, besides the faculty members and professors, Krsek invited and welcomed representatives of the unions, the Communist Party and, most importantly, the Communist students, who turned out to be the most aggressive and vocal force on the scene. Advancements were now issued to junior professors and "politically correct" lecturers were advanced the rank of full professor, thus jumping two steps ahead in the academic ranks. Lecturers Karol Šiška, Jozef Černáček, Žikmund Križan, Ivan Hečko, Július P. Tóth, Vladimír Vršanský and Ján Kubis, among others, became the new flag-bearers at the Medical School, most of the Czechoslovakists, Communists, and Protestants.

The regular meetings of this mixed bag of faculty members convened at the Dean's office and had the distinct character of a political rally rather than a meeting to deal with the real problems of the Medical School. In the case of a political event in the city or country, such as a meeting of the Central Committee of the Communist Party in Prague, or Stalin's birthday, an extraordinary meeting would be called to celebrate the event.

The ultimate goal was to revamp the Medical School based on the Soviet model. However, this was wishful thinking because no one really had a realistic opportunity or the time to study the structure, advantages or foibles of this visionary ideal, since the political masters strove for immediate change at any cost! The other goal was to remake the professorial body by removing the members who were still suspect, but also by attrition, easing out the older generation suspected of political opportunism who disguised their reticence about the new model. Only those were retained who were the most devoted or trustworthy (or corrupt) senior members who would catalyze and advance the frontal attack of the new postwar medical graduates—the Communist avant-garde who would accomplish the political revolution and reform. A final, but not less important, goal was to revamp the student body at the Medical School by means of thorough political and social engineering, using the wide-spread democratization process which was the sinister cloak for the removal of students who lacked the ideological convictions and enthusiasm for the new political canon.

In order to achieve a thorough ideological re-education at the Medical School, a Chair of Marxism-Leninism was born and an era of lavish political slogans commenced. The Communist Party would lead, influence and dictate, with Dialectical Materialism as the only scientific foundation of any science. This double-headed monster was now introduced in compulsory lectures each semester as the main ingredient of any discipline where an ideological point of view had to be blended into the medical curricula. The difficulty was that the political transformation was so radical that not enough qualified tutors with in-depth knowledge about this new ideological revelation sprang forth within the Communist Party to present a credible theory or discipline. Nevertheless, at faculty meetings, under the aegis of Drs. Krsek and Dérer, the discussions were saturated by this political mantra so that other professors would incorporate them into their lectures as well. The Marxist ideologue during these faculty meetings was Dr. Šimon Svitek and very soon the junior Dr. J. Gero followed suit.

Dr. Šimon Svitek (1895–1970) had an interesting political history. In 1918, as a 23-year-old, he joined the Hungarian Communist Party and was a member of the Red Army in 1919 during the Communist uprising led by Béla Kun, who seized power in Hungary and southern Slovakia. For this he was later imprisoned in Szombathely (Hungary). He graduate from Charles IV University's Medical School (Prague) in 1924 and practiced medicine until 1949. From 1929 he was chairman of the leftist front in Czechoslovakia and during the Slovak Republic he was jailed but escaped before being sent to a concentration camp. From 1949 he held various high-ranking political positions, eventually becoming a lecturer at the Political School of the Central Committee of the Communist Party. In the late 1960's he received many political awards and the Medal of Honor in 1965 for his political work.[6]

These professors insisted that the Marxist-Leninist ideology of the Communist Party was the only relevant one, and the slogan, "The Soviet Union, our shining example," was extolled *ad nauseam*. It is interesting to read the minutes of these meeting which reveal how they, establish professors, competed amongst themselves in trying to outdo each other in this political display and theater. Dr. J. Černáček personally lauded Stalin—no mean feat—as showing the correct path towards the future (in medicine?). Did he really mean it?[7]

Dr. V. Vršanský, the biology lecturer, could not praise the importance of ideological education enough. This man who, just two years earlier in Zurich had learned to stain the chromosomes of the Mediterranean fruit fly, now rejected the cellular theory of life. Without any doubt or misgiving, he accepted the word of the Rasputin of Soviet biology, Trofim Lysenko, that genes do not exist, accepting instead his claims regarding acellular "living matter," which were totally unsubstantiated and unscientific. Vršanský, of course, scored political points when he abandoned the genetics of Gregor Mendel, the Benedictine monk who had germinated his peas in a monastery only a hundred miles away, and his American apostle, Dr. J. Morgan of Columbia University in New York.

The ever-present Ján Gero, a neophyte doctor, lectured his colleagues on the teachings of I. P. Pavlov, which the Soviets mechanistically vulgarized, regarding the higher neural functions of the brain organized as an upstairs-downstairs theater. Dr. Dérer exhorted the faculty: "We have to understand the dialectic, the art of reasoning correctly, in its methodology." The audience was stunned because no one had a clue what he was talking about and no one dared ask whether even *he* understood what he was talking about.

As the IX Communist Party Congress convened on May 25–29, 1949, Gero hastened to underline the professors' tasks and consequently their commitments:

> We have to both study the conclusions of the Central Committee, and study Marxism-Leninism with involvement in order to struggle for world peace, just as J. Stalin and K. Gottwald, the Party General Secretary and the President, encouraged, as well as fight against western propaganda and the warmongering of the USA.[8]

The 1950's brought a wave of purges from the Central Committee against the ideological aberrations of the Slovaks, the so-called struggle against "bourgeois nationalism." The Czech Communists attacked the nationalism of the Slovaks when the latter aspired for equality of power with their Czech comrades and questioned the ideology of "democratic centralism." With this clever slogan, Prague's Communists seized the upper hand in the leadership of the Party for a group of a few privileged Czechs. The deprecating coinage "bourgeois" introduced the element of class struggle into this contest, which was the kiss of death for the Slovaks. What "bourgeois' actually meant was that some of the leading Slovak Communists had a higher education and were of middle-class origins, and some of them really were. Consequently, Novomeský and some of his cronies such as Dr. G. Husák were jailed for many years while Dr. V. Clementis, the Foreign Secretary, was hanged. Accordingly, in Prague there was no Czech "bourgeois nationalism."

At the Ministry of Education, Novomeský was replaced by another ardent Communist, comrade E. Sýkora. He finalized and formalized the political changes at the University by introducing law number 58 of May 18, 1950, by which the whole higher education system was changed in its structure, organization, and form according to the Soviet model. His speech introducing this law was published in the Communist daily *Pravda* (Truth) on May 21, 1950 (vol. 31, No. 118, p. 3) under the heading, "For the Marxist-Leninist Education at the University" (Fig. 3.3). Sýkora now led the attack against the "old guard" of the remaining professors at the University and challenged them with his political exhortations: "We can't just have professors at the University who only have sympathies for the new political order, socialistic science and socialism. We have to have people who will build a bastion of Marxism-Leninism and be involved in the mortal struggle against the remnants of the reactionary bourgeois and religion." He urged the Communist student avant-garde, the members of the Czechoslovak youth organization equipped with the theory of Marxism-Leninism and in brotherhood with the working class, to stamp out the rest of the bourgeois nationalists and expel the reactionary forces from their positions. It was a declaration of ideological war! His speech, of course, was echoed at the Medical School faculty meeting during the presentation of Dr. K. Šiška, soon to be a member of the Central Committee, who parroted the entire harangue, adding his own twist: "We must be vigilant because the capitalists are mounting a deadly attack on our struggle to build socialism in our land."[9]

As a consequence of this sanguine challenge by the Minister, the political attack by the student body was not long in coming. The medical students did not want to be outdone by Sýkora and therefore organized a mammoth meeting, or "activ" as it was called. The meeting was called by the student organization and held in the festive graduation hall of the University in May 1950. The entire faculty was required to be present at this charade.

The Minister of Education himself, E. Sýkora, was seated on the dais, flanked by the most aggressive and strident avant-garde headed by its main actors, V. Zvara, D. Brucháč, E. Breuer, M. Toldy, E. Huraj, J. Rosival, B. Brozman, J. Lahita and some opportunistic acolytes such as J. Baranyai, A. Biro and others students. The galleries were crammed with students in support of their professors who loathed the new gang of political upstarts.

The main introductory remarks were made by the Minister of Education himself. The Minister, a political parvenu, naturally encouraged the students to be frank and to the point. The criticism and attacks of these young Communist posers was harsh, ruthless and personal. The students, especially those who had already muddled through their respective exams, assailed their teachers with a vengeance, besmirching their personal honor and dignity.

One of the first speakers was V. Zvara, who was known for his fierce looks and disposition. He had just passed the Communal Hygiene exam and wanted to get even with his examiner, Professor V. Mucha. His emotions barely in check, in a shrill tenor he accused Mucha of glorifying the U.S. health care system without mentioning the slums of Harlem, or the eight million unemployed, thus showing his pro-U.S. bias and therefore, being a liar. Zvara continued that Mucha seemed to forget that the U.S. was bracing for war against the Soviet Union and he was supporting its military machine, making him therefore a warmonger. And how do you compare fascism with Marxism-Leninism, Zvara asked, when it gave us both Lenin and Stalin? How can this teacher with his cosmopolitan views educate a new generation of physicians for the people's democracy? Zvara demanded. Mucha was obviously shaken by the savage attack by a junior, half his age, with no in-depth knowledge of medical matters. While he blushed and almost sobbed, Mucha banged on his wooden leg, a result of a wound sustained in the First World War, and exclaimed, "How can I be a warmonger when I lost my leg in the war?"

Dr. J. Tréger, Professor of Dermatology, received a scathing censure from his junior associate, Dr. Chmell, and his comrades Drs. Rehák and Hegyi, and was labeled totally incompetent in teaching, research and organization. The poor man died a few months later while Rehák used the Party springboard to have uncontested career, achieving his ultimate ambition of becoming a Soviet-style Academician.

The founder of Slovak surgery, Professor Dr. K. Čársky, was denounced by the medical student Szanto and his younger associate in surgery, Dr. M. Kratochvil. Kratochvil charged that during these new political times Čársky still pursued his private practice, that he promulgated an idealistic philosophy and sometimes relied on his intuition and not on scientific knowledge and evidence. Therefore, he was unfit to be the Chairman of the Department of Surgery. Šársky was flabbergasted that his trainee would stab him in the back with such absurd accusations, but with tears in his eyes, he was unable to utter a word.

The political bigwig, D. Brucháč, hurled similar criticisms against Professor Dr. J. Žucha, one of the outstanding surgeons of the Medical School and the founder of pediatric and later brain surgery. Žucha returned to Slovakia from Prague by invitation of Professor Dr. E. Filo. He had studied brain surgery in Stockholm with the world famous Professor Dr. Olivercrona and was one of his favorite students. Žucha, a handsome, over six-feet tall athlete with a receding blond hairline and sky-blue eyes, was accused of being an aristocrat because of his nonchalant and elegant behavior, even though he was the son of a doorman. He was accused of a lack of enthusiasm for the new political system and had made some mocking remarks regarding its less-than-illustrious Communist members. His lack of attention to Soviet literature and journals was another failing. Dr. J. Červenanský, the country's leading orthopedist, was accused by his junior associate-to-be, Dr. E. Huraj, of accepting bribes from a blue-collar worker.

The most harshly targeted was the Chairman of the Department of Anatomy, Dr. E. Šteklacová. She was a terse but objective examiner, and many of her mediocre Communist students repeatedly failed to measure up. She was also one of the professors who intertwined her lectures with some moral intimations and reminders to the students, and underscored the importance of professional integrity, honesty and rectitude in the sense of the Hippocratic ideals. These teachings were, of course, in total contradiction to the philosophy and practice of the new wave of Communist students amongst whom, under a derelict political ideology, flagrant personal interest, opportunism and ruthless aspirations carried the day. Dr. Šteklacová was severely criticized for her unflinching ideals and her days at the Medical School were numbered.

It was a moment of high drama when the most aggressive accusation was made against one of the most respected and beloved professors of Pathology, Dr. Frank Klein. His attacker was Emil Belica, a senior student who had just managed to pass his pathology exam.

Belica's vitriolic and ignoble calumny focused on Dr. Klein's allegiance to the classical European pathology of R. Wirchow, the founder of this discipline, and also to his cellular vitalist interpretation, and Klein's avoidance of attention to Soviet pathology and its achievements.

Klein was always ready with a prompt and blunt reply. Everyone expected it at this show and students in the galleries stomped their feet in support of him. He lifted his husky figure and climbed up the dais with his wobbly, broad-based gait. Through his heavy black-framed spectacles, his dark eyes regarded Belica and his henchmen with appreciable contempt and he retorted in his booming baritone: "I never harmed Mr. Belica; he just recently squeaked through his exam in pathology. But I know that he is nothing but a mouthpiece or a well-rehearsed gramophone record and he only parrots things which he was told to say." Applause, jeers, bursts of laughter and stomping came from the audience. Klein aimed his remarks at his appointed associate, the Communist M. Brozman, who eventually became his nemesis and successor:

> I have nothing to apologize for! I am an old Jew and I suffered through the war like a dog. Yes, I claim allegiance to R. Wirchow because he is the best. The same R. Wirchow who in the German Parliament during the First World War stood up for the poor and the hungry. And anyway I don't know any Soviet pathologist comparable to Wirchow!

The whole auditorium erupted in pandemonium in support of this courageous man and the applause died down slowly. The Communists on the dais were beaten. A young Jewish student and ardent Communist, W. Bauer, raised his objections against the laudatory approval of Klein but he was quickly hushed and Klein carried the day.[10]

In 1952, Dean Stanek dared to voice his concerns about the chaos in the teaching plans and that the students were memorizing the theory of Marxism-Leninism by rote instead of intelligently interpreting its gospel. As a consequence, Dr. Dérer responded by criticizing the passivity of the older generation of professors and pointed to their ideological disorientation and how it should be overcome by listening to Stalin, reading his pamphlet (which turned out to be plagiarized) and teaching about his linguistic theory in science.

Suddenly a big event overshadowed everything at the Medical School when Dr. Šiška welcomed the Moscow academician Birjukov, a pupil of I. P. Pavlov. "This is the model of a real Soviet man," extolled Dr. Šiška, "critical, straight and friendly." However, Birjukov's professional achievements or specialties were not mentioned.

In the following meetings of the faculty, Dr. Vršanský again excelled when he extolled the virtues of the Marxist-Leninist ideology that was supposed to advance all scientific endeavors. Dr. Krsek explained again the Communist Party would show the Medical School (!) the correct path from now on and that Academician Černáček would educate the other members of the faculty about the essence of Marxist-Leninist science. Nevertheless, Dr. Vršanský again emphasized that the medical intelligentsia had to be dedicated to the working class and to the "people's democracy" using the help of Marxism-Leninism and the materialistic foundations of medical science. Dr. T. R. Niederland counseled for the need for mastery of the Russian language as an integral part of ideological conversion and the necessity of supervision of the medical curriculum and its results by the CSM, the Communist youth organization.

This merry-go-round of political mottos and exhortations had no end. Psychiatrist Dr. E. Guensberger fired a big salvo, claiming that Dialectic Materialism was the essence of most scientific achievements and knowledge, while the Communist priestess J. Michaličková invoked Lenin himself about the three types of intellectuals: the good for nothing, the reactionary but correctable, and the devoted who won the day!

But clouds were gathering on the horizon and it was again Dean Stanek who vented his spleen by pointing out that the working and personal relationships between senior professors and the new assistant professors was less than desirable. The old guard didn't support the new Communist avant-garde and these new gladiators didn't respect the old. What he really meant was the "Young Turks" were out to get the positions of the old professors, trampling down anyone who got in their way.

In the mid-1950's, as he had wished, Dr. L. Dérer finally achieved the coveted Soviet degree of Academician. Even though it was not really his field or forte, he established a research laboratory in conjunction with the Slovak Academy of Sciences, following in the footsteps of I. P. Pavlov, studying higher neural functions, a pet project of the Soviets.

At this time Dérer was repeatedly and suspiciously absent from faculty meetings. The reason for his withdrawal—a well-kept secret—was that he had been struggling for years with severe bouts of alcoholism which significantly compromised his ability to function. One has to wonder what kinds of ghosts were haunting him after leaving his mark on and compromising the lives of so many professional colleagues. A stomach cancer was discovered soon after in 1960 Dr. K. Dérer had to end his earthly journey and face his Creator.

To this very day, Dérer remains the most revered physician of the Medical School and of the country, and the main University Hospital carries his name. There is stony silence regarding his political activities and his clout, which destroyed a great many professional and personal lives.

In the final twist of political subterfuge emulating the Soviet model, the managing structure of the individual departments at the Medical School was changed and the process of academic advancement was altered. New, imported, and odd-sounding academic titles were introduced for the different levels of academic progress, such as Candidate of Science, followed by Doctor of Science, titles never before used at institutions of higher education. These new degrees were now the prerequisites for the rank of Lecturer or Professor. The pinnacle of professorial status at the Medical School—the coveted title of Academician—was yearned for in order to achieve parity with the Soviet academicians and comrades.

According to the Soviet model, the individual departments were split into new sub-units or Chairs called "Cathedra," assigned mainly to teaching and headed by a Secretary of the Cathedra. This way more room and control was given to the young Communist Assistant Professors who, with their fingers on the pulse of the department, kept the Professors who led the research in check while still running the rest of the business of the division. Having become figureheads within the departments, the senior Professors were totally paralyzed and frustrated, since the secretaries of the Cathedra, as politically-correct successors, continued to take care of their own interests, working hand-in-hand with the Communist Party and functioned as the new shadow government of the Medical School. This dual and cumbersome structure led to significant tensions within the divisions and further polarized the allegiances of the department members with one group being the professors while the others were on the side of the secretary. Needless to say, even the most politically correct professors were unhappy when these medical neophytes, most at the very beginning of their chosen academic careers, were breathing down their necks.

Still, these new pioneers of the Soviet model and science had to be hatched and so in the early 1950's only this elite group of Communists could aspire to the first step on the academic ladder by becoming a Candidate of Science. A document virtually unknown to others regarding these candidates lets us peek into these surreptitious affairs and indicates that in the academic year 1951/52, eleven of these illustrious comrades were chosen by themselves and the Party to go to the best institutions for advanced training. They were sent to Prague to train in different specialties, which they could choose themselves. No one else from the Medical School had this privilege except these comrades.

It should be stressed that a critical step in the process of earning the degree of Candidate of Science—which was only later opened to other assistant professors—was to participate in compulsory courses in Russian and indoctrination in Marxist-Leninist political science. A postdoctoral thesis was then produced which had to be submitted for review or be contested by two opponents or judges of medical merit. This was a severely flawed and politically tainted academic process that no one dared, or even cared, to contest, let alone address, since the advancement to Candidates of Sciences for this group of Communists was a foregone conclusion.

Only in the late 1950's and 60's could other mortals such as assistant professors join this process of academic advancement, but working only locally at the Medical School. Most of the postdoctoral theses of later years were written without any funding and with great difficulty because of a lack of technology and comprehensive literary resources. The works were basically literary overviews of existing problems with some modification of original ideas already published, found and adapted mostly from American journals. After achieving this milestone the Candidate received a monthly stipend of 300 crowns, equal to 10 US dollars for Sisyphean work which lasted a minimum of three years. A staggering number—some 3,500 works of this kind—was produced over 40 years at the Medical School, about 90 per academic year. Aside from their value as a local diploma, these works did not make any appreciable impact on, or advancement of, medical science or the practice of medicine.[11]

After the Communist elite picked their specialties and achieved the Candidate of Science degree, they were awarded the position of a state lecturer by the Ministry of Education with the blessing of the Communist Party. The race for further advancement in academia was then on. Faithfully adhering to the Soviet model, the avant-garde pursued its next goal: becoming a Doctor of Science. Again in the mid-1950's and 60's, only the flag-bearers or the cream of the new Communist doctors could be assigned this coveted title which automatically led them to the rank of Professor. A strong injection of Marxist indoctrination was again very much part of this endeavor. The process and requirements of this degree were that a somewhat longer and more advanced dissertation was required, incorporating some degree of originality. But again, most of the time medical technology and resources comparable to what was accessible for Ph.D. study in the West and particularly in the U.S. were simply not available. A financial monthly stipend for this degree was 1,000 crowns, the equivalent of about 35 US dollars. This is a meaningful example of the value medical science had in the eyes of the political authorities. About 260 Doctors of Science graduated in 40 years, which is about seven graduates per year at the Medical School, serving a population of about 4 million—a figure more indicative of the high quantity of research rather than its quality.[12]

By Western standards these works were significantly compromised by the political background of the graduates of that time. The patron professor of the nominee had a vested interest that the chosen Communist scientist's work would pass the peer review of five. Because of the political credentials of the candidate, especially in the early years, as a rule he or she passed and was awarded the degree of Doctor of Science, Soviet style. After the first revolutionary wave, when all the top places were occupied by this avant-garde, this degree became available for other, less fervent, political appointees.

A state-appointed professorship usually followed the achievement of the Doctor of Science degree, along with the inheritance of departmental fiefdoms. At this stage, the most ambitious professors strove for the Soviet-style academic Olympus by becoming an Academician. The aspiring Chairmen and Professors established working relationships in the clinical disciplines or basic sciences with the departments of the Slovak Academy of Science, where they were welcomed by their old cronies. The latter were funded directly by the government and the Party and not by the Medical School and were willing to lend a helping hand to combine clinical and applied research, since they had better technology. In this manner the professors from the Medical School received an appointment at the Academy of Sciences and were then nominated to be a Corresponding Member, a Soviet title, and ultimately an Academician as the endpoint of this circuitous scientific-political endeavor to be equal or in the same category or level as their Soviet counterparts. It was not enough for these teachers and professors at the Medical School to remain in their domain of teaching the future generation of doctors, as most Western professors are happy and proud to do. Emulating the Soviet model, they wanted something more.

In twenty years this social engineering completely reshuffled the entire Medical Faculty and achieved a Soviet model which brought about a totally new, untested medical system with hitherto unknown and unexpected outcomes whose results were supposed to be safeguarded and affirmed by the new Communist mantra of Marxism-Leninism.

In the mid-1970's, after my own rigorous retraining in pediatric cardiology at Boston's Children's Hospital, I bade farewell to this illustrious institution and to my mentor with a heavy heart. My chief, and now friend for life, a professor at Harvard Medical School, also had roots in Europe, and also had fled before another "ism." At the small farewell party, he approached me mischievously saying, "Tell me, Zoltan, what would I have to do to become an Academician in the Soviet Union?" In my startled reaction to this unexpected and surprising question, I blurted out, "Well, I think as a first step you would have to join the Communist Party." His reply was quick and to the point, "No, thank you!"

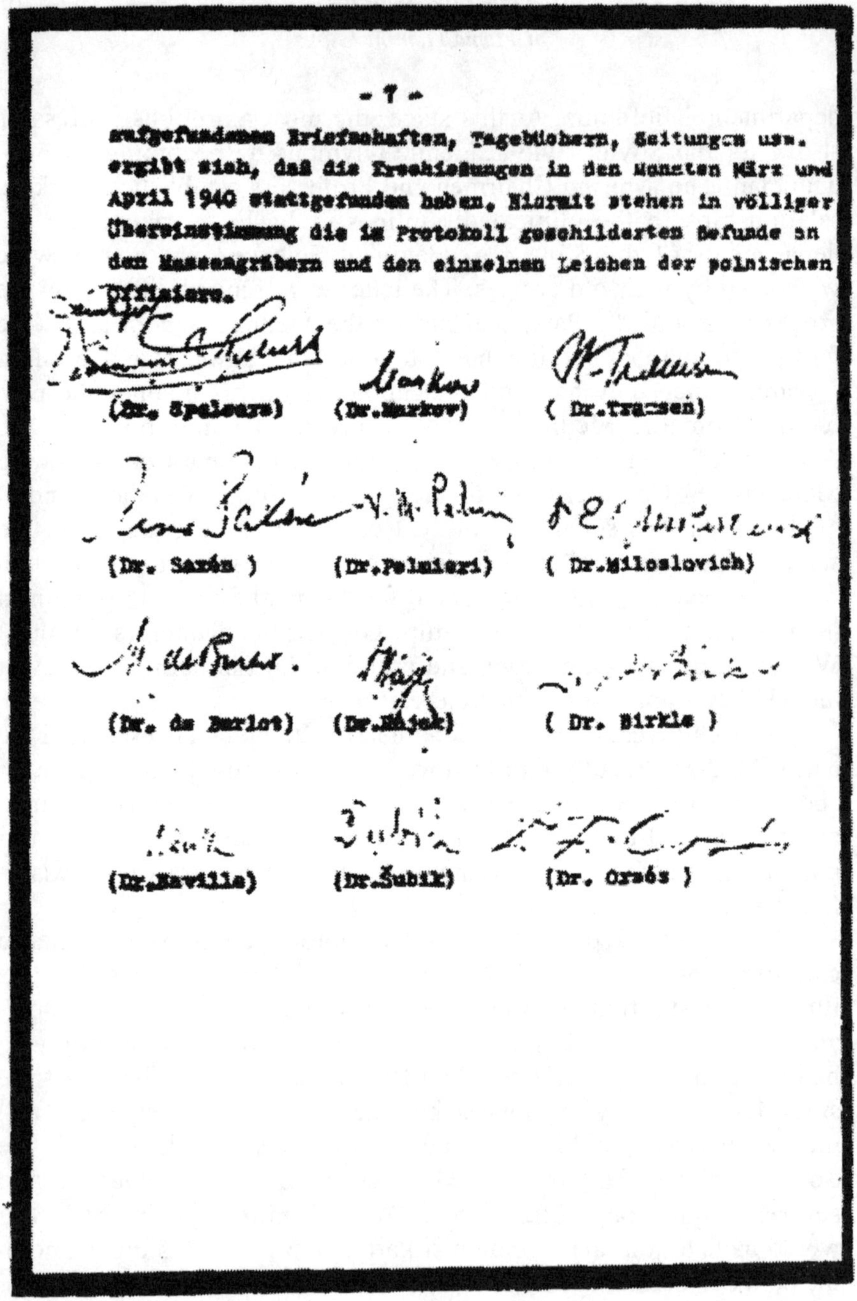
- 7 -

aufgefundenen Briefschaften, Tagebüchern, Zeitungen usw. ergibt sich, daß die Erschießungen in den Monaten März und April 1940 stattgefunden haben. Hiermit stehen in völliger Übereinstimmung die im Protokoll geschilderten Befunde an den Massengräbern und den einzelnen Leichen der polnischen Offiziere.

(Dr. Speleers) (Dr. Markov) (Dr. Tramsen)

(Dr. Saxén) (Dr. Palmieri) (Dr. Miloslovich)

(Dr. de Burlet) (Dr. Hájek) (Dr. Birkle)

(Dr. Naville) (Dr. Šubik) (Dr. Orsós)

Fig. 3.1: Signatures of the forensic-medical experts at the massacre in Katyń, Poland, 1941

Fig. 3.2
"Action Committee" of the University students and professors, 1948

ÚSTREDNÝ AKČNÝ VÝBOR
VYSOKOŠKOLSKÉHO ŠTUDENSTVA
V BRATISLAVE

predseda   Ján Zelinka
podpredseda   Jozef Fraňo
II. podpredseda   Stanislav Bahurinský
tajomnik   Dušan Brucháč
členovia:Slavomir Repáč, Timotej Turský, Dr.
Veselý, Andrej Sulety, Július Gašparík, Pavol
Krnáš, Ivan Šurina, Ján Šimovčík, Milan Matula, Rudolf Turňa, Vladimir Čech, Darina Barac-
ková, Mária Janzová, Stanislav Klaučo, J. Jed-
nák, Pavel Pollák, Ján Májek, Frant. Figura
(Prevzaté z časopisu: Borba, ročnik II. č 11.
z. 10. 3. 1948)

ÚSTREDNÝ VÝBOR NÁRODNÉHO FRONTU
NA VYSOKÝCH ŠKOLÁCH
ustanovený 3. Marca 1948 v. Bratislave

predseda   Prof. Dr. Lukáč
podpredseda   Prof. Dr. Mráz
tajomnik   Dr. Czambel
členovia: Prof. Dr. Bakoš, Prof. Dr. Isačenko,
Prof. Dr. Krsek, Prof. Červeňanský, Prof. Dr.
Černáček, Prof. Dr. Vanovič, Prof. Ing. Gonda,
Prof. Ing. Dr. Havelka, Prof. Dr. Krempaský, Prof.
Ing. Dr. Cicvárek, Dr. Dubnický, Dr. Šuster, Dr.
Schvarz, Ing. Golier, Ing. Šimovič.
zo študentov: Ján Zelinka, Jozef Fraňo, Mária
Janzová, Milan Matula, Timotej Turský, Viťazo-
slav Petráš, Dušan Brucháč, Stanislav Bahurinský, Andrej Sulety.

Za marx-leninskú výchovu vysokoškolákov

Prejav povereníka E. Sýkoru na aktíve bratislavských vysokoškolákov — funkcionárov ČSM

(z) B r a t i s l a v a — Študenti bratislavských vysokých škôl na aktíve funkcionárov ČSM, ktorý bol 19. mája, zhodnotili doterajšiu prácu socializácii vysokých škôl. V širokej diskusii vyslovili sa za dôsledné odišu v radoch študentov i profesorov, ktorí si doposiaľ nevedeli osvojiť pokrokové tendencie, prenikajúce na vysoké školy a uchovávajú zrôzne prežitky na tomto dôležitom úseku. Na aktíve zúčastnil sa aj predseda SÚV ČSM povereník školstva, vied a umení Ernest Sýkora a mohí členovia profesorského sboru.

Fig. 3.3: "For a Marxist-Leninist education at the University!"
The title of the speech of the Communist Secretary of Education,
Comrade Ernest Sykora, May, 1950

4
Democratization of the Students or
Social Engineering, Soviet Style

The Merriam Webster Collegiate Dictionary (1993) defines democracy as government by the people or rule by the majority. Even in the bulkiest encyclopedia there is no mention of the word "democratization," which was an invention of the times by the politically correct elite after 1948 in Communist-ruled Czechoslovakia. Democratization of the student body at the University or the Medical School was nothing but a sinister coinage, or dare I say, an example of the perversion of the democratic process where a minority of the students, a clique anointed by the Communist Party, sought the elimination of the ideological enemy. The enemy of this elite, the majority of whom had joined the Communist Party in 1948, were their own classmates, who were systematically accused on drummed-up charges of disloyalty to the new political establishment when most of these students were at worst apolitical—a liability indeed in those times. These students had come to school, after all, to study medicine, not political science.

Members of the Sicilian Mafia were poor neophytes compared to this Communist clan which used its membership in the Communist Party to eliminate their fellow classmates, leaving a clear field for themselves to choose coveted specialties or positions in different institutions. They had their eyes already on professorships in a Communist empire with no end in sight.

After graduation, these privileged few forged a political network and became the shadow government at the Medical School with the blessing of the Communist Party that they now virtually owned. The new slogan was, "Hail to the studentocracy!"

In the heyday of the Communist revolution in February 1948, the Communist-controlled daily *Praca* (Work) exhorted the prospective mothers of the land: "We have to be sure that our progeny will be nursed only the red milk of pristine Communism, thus this new generation will develop into a new Communist avant-garde!" In Prague V. Kopecký, the Communist ideologue, issued a tirade for the new generation: "Our society doesn't need an intelligentsia, their university will be the daily reading of the *Rudé Pravo* [Red Right—the daily of the Central Committee of the Communist Party]." The prime target of the Communists in Bratislava was first and foremost the entire Catholic student body and its elite residing in the Catholic dormitory of Svoradov. The Minister of Education, L. Novomeský, proclaimed furiously in 1947: "...and we will conquer this Catholic Alcazar!"[1]

To start, the authorities dismissed the administration of the dormitory on the spot without any notice and appointed a Communist high school teacher, Rudolf Lakáč, as the director. He was politically bolstered by an Action Committee of senior Communist students. Subsequently, the spiritual counselors, the priests, were dismissed, followed by the expulsion of the elevated Vincentian nuns. In a final blow, the chapel was closed and later dismantled.

From 1947 on, the Catholic student body was surreptitiously infiltrated by non-Catholic students of Protestant and Jewish faith and Czechoslovak political persuasion, as well as by Communists and former partisans, participants in the Slovak Uprising of 1944. A spiritual eclipse descended over this community of students who were the Catholic sons of humble origins. This cloud cast a dark shadow of intimidation and fear over the very fabric of their daily life. Now, new faces appeared on the scene with strange expressions and searching, penetrating eyes—men with stiff and uncomfortable posture who always seemed to be snooping around this formerly serene place and its community. These extraterrestrials wanted to gaze into our souls and discover our innermost thoughts. Who were these grim, poker-faced aliens, who tried to avoid eye contact, turning their heads when addressed? It slowly dawned on us that this was the new Communist avant-garde who had the task of infiltrating, disrupting, and ultimately destroying the community of the student dorms. "Svoradov delenda est!" was their battle cry—"Svoradov must be destroyed!" These strangers walked together and associated in groups, and kept to their own kind.

A duo of Communist students, Vladimír Zvara and Ivan Litvaj, were quite conspicuous from the start. Zvara was a tall, handsome fellow, a medical student with dark brown curly hair and strangely protruding eyes that looked as if he wanted to unveil your thoughts and ideas. Litvaj, a student of economics, was a shorter, cock-eyed blond fellow who always kept his gaze on the ground. He was known to be a Communist zealot and former partisan and was later trained in Moscow and became most influential in the Central Committee of the Communist Party at the University and of the government. His lifeline to the Communist Party was his wife, E. Chuľková, originally a blue-collar worker and a genuine Communist, a lifelong member of the Party, and later even a member of Parliament. Another member of this group was a medical student, Ján Gero. His name, originally Hungarian, Gerő, had been adjusted for Slovak consumption. Interestingly, in Hungary he had a namesake, Ernő Gerő, a prominent Jewish Communist who was one of the culprits who triggered the Hungarian Revolution in 1956. Another prominent Communist student was Martin Lúčan, a former partisan who climbed up the political ladder with the speed of light, and soon became the Secretary of the Central Committee of the Communist Party and Chairman of the Department of Marxism-Leninism; he later became Minister of Education and finally Vice Premier in the government.

But this zealous elite was soon joined by local turncoats from the dorm such as Ján Ziman, Martin Drobný, Jozef Zachar, and man others who took the opportunity to jump on the Communist bandwagon to advance their careers. The goal of the Communists was the reeducation of the willing and the intimidation, with the ultimate elimination, of the stubborn and faithful who stuck to their convictions. Their marching orders were to destroy the enemy. They were specifically interested in students with religious convictions and faith—the "clericals," as they were cynically labeled—who were nothing but decent students of moral fiber and principles, personal character and honor which reflected their origins and the majority of Catholics in the land. These students were regarded as the worst political and ideological enemy because they pledged their allegiance to the Catholic Church—the main, if not the only, bastion against the onslaught of Communism.

Immediately after the "Victorious February" of 1948, regular weekend conferences for reeducation of students started with great fanfare in the auditorium of the dorm where everyone was invited for an introductory political lecture followed by discussions of the participants. The ultimate goal of these rallies was mainly to uncover, and eventually to weed out, so-called "reactionary elements" and their intellectual chieftains.

The lecture hall, painted sky blue, accommodated about 150 students and the reeducators on the dais were Communist lecturers mainly from the University School of Philosophy and Law. In key positions within the audience, the new Communist students were planted as observers and moles to monitor and follow every move of the "reactionary" Catholics and to take notice of who was talking and what was being said. Fierce and highly intellectual philosophical, political and religious battles developed between the presiding Communist elite and the senior students of the dorm who, as gladiators ready to perish, attacked this political wolf pack. The main target and bone of contention in this Catholic milieu were the pros and cons of atheism, which was extolled by the lecturers, while religion—the opium of the people—was ridiculed, deeply offending the majority of the audience.

On at least two of the evenings in the spring of 1948, Dr. Karol Rebro, a bespectacled man of medium frame, in his late thirties, with neatly combed light chestnut hair, attended. It was the same man who, after the war, chaired the certifying commissions where many members of the Medical School were sacrificed to political mandates. After shattering many illustrious careers, he now came to continue his sinister work among the Slovak Catholic students. In his presentation, he extolled the ideology of Marxism as the only scientific philosophy and on this soil, deliberately and provocatively denigrated the Catholic Church. A ferocious exchange erupted between him and the students of Svoradov who handed him a humiliating defeat—after a four-hour long battle, he packed his attaché case and amidst explosive jeering, left the auditorium annoyed and flustered.

Tragically, but not unexpectedly, as a consequence of this "triumph" by the Catholic students, at 7 a.m. in the lobby of the dorm there appeared a neatly typed list of students pinned to the bulletin board—the "victors" of the previous night, who were now to be expelled or "democratized" from the University.

* * *

In the midst of this turbulent spring, we knew there would be huge political rally on May 1st—the first workers' day celebration under the Communist rule of the country. The whole city was turned red by banners bearing the hammer and sickle. Stern instructions were issued that all members of governmental organizations, schools, factories, former partisans and peoples' militia would march through the city in a major parade to celebrate and hail the Communist Party and the Soviet Union, our shining example, and declare death to the reactionary forces—all this before a presiding gallery of political luminaries.

Ominously, our dorm—the mutinous Svoradov—had to be ready in a platoon and in a line of ten students abreast, ready, spick-and-span in our best suits, and with strong vocal cords. Many banners and billboards were prepared to show off this "Catholic Alcazar" in its new colors in support of the Communist regime. A day before the rally I received a message to report to the administration. Having a bad premonition, I reported immediately and a group of us, mostly in the second semester, were ushered into a small conference room. Nobody knew what was going on and everybody smelled a rat.

A most unpleasant and noted proletarian comrade, Ján Jedinák, stood before us like a drill sergeant and informed us in no uncertain terms that we had been given the honor of carrying and displaying the different banners in front of and within the platoon of the student body during the May 1st parade. All of us were regulars of Svoradov, while no Communist student had received this coveted distinction. We were flabbergasted and in an uproar about this abuse, but this sinister rogue let it be known that there would be no exceptions from this duty and whoever refused would be expelled from the dorm and the University as a class enemy. We left like beaten dogs, knowing that there was no way out of this trap.

I had nightmares, tossing in my bed the entire night. Nevertheless I had to report to the courtyard before 7 a.m. to take on this humiliation. I was with my good friend and classmate, V.B., who was one of the most decent human beings I have ever met and who was later jailed for his religious beliefs, when a huge banner was pressed into our hands. The tow us in a last ditch effort tried to sneak to the tail of the student column assembled on the street but one of the Communist goons grabbed us and pushed us smack in front of the main student body. We were so ashamed and humiliated that our eyes welled up with tears at this devastating predicament.

We marched with the banner at the level of our chins so that no one could recognize us in this ignoble situation. With our view thus obstructed, we stumbled more than once on the cobblestones of Bratislava. We shuffled with heavy hearts, carrying the banner emblazoned with the words, "Forever with the Soviet Union." But somehow after the long hours of the march through the main streets of the town a defiant pride rose in our bosoms because it was *our* dorm, which we were leading. We especially felt this pride regarding our Svoradov as we approached the government platform where about a hundred Communist leaders were lined up in rows on the dais, sitting and watching this perverse and regimented parade. As our platoon approached the platform, the red elite of the students ordered the student body to chant and roar, praising the Communist Party, the Soviet Union, and their founding fathers. Repetitious outbursts and applause on command were heard from the distance up until our dorm reached the scene.

Despite all orders and intimidation, this Catholic elite of tall and handsome youth, ramrod straight with stiff upper lips, all dressed in dark overcoats and black neckties, grew even taller at this defiant moment. Erect, with bulging chests, we didn't utter one word for these proletarian henchmen! We marched in stony silence like a solemn phalanx of gladiators on their final march! As I glanced to the right of the platform, I could see the Communist Party Secretary, Viliam Široký, crestfallen and shocked while his surrounding gang was jumping up from their seats, yelling, "What's going on? Who are these stony-faced men?" because me we had now become! We eventually passed the platform and moved into a large square where people were dispersing. Together with my friend, we turned into small side street and smashed the hated banner onto the ground, breaking it into pieces and finally running and hiding among the crowd. We were very much concerned about the possible reprisals following this debacle, but the

Communists eventually glossed over this episode in the glow of their political triumph even though we all knew that we were now on their blacklist.

* * *

A few weeks later, in June, parliamentary elections were to be held—basically a political charade. There were only two options: to vote for the so-called National Front (the Communists), or against it. The majority of the students of Svoradov wanted to vote against the Communist Party in this secret ballot, but they smelled a rat. On the day of the elections when the ballots were supposed to be cast in the lecture hall of the dorm, we were all tense and nervous. In the corridors of the dorm the senior students discussed a strategy of how to proceed and assessed the battle plan and its potential consequences. How naive we all were! Everyone examined the ballot cards, turning them around, analyzing the paper, even smelling it. Then a chemistry student had the idea to scan the ballot card over the light bulb of his desk lamp. The strong light revealed nothing irregular but the heat emanating from the bulb displayed a four-digit number written with invisible ink. The shock of this revelation spread through the dorm like wildfire: we were outraged at this obvious entrapment. The Communists wanted to penetrate even the privacy of our hearts and minds to descry in us the "reactionary enemy."

Some senior students went to the proctors at the voting boxes and showed them this illegal ruse. The Communist guardians made the ridiculous excuse that during the night someone had broken into the safe and labeled the cards. Some of the students went to the police station to get new ballots in a futile attempt to exchange their cards. It was obvious that the entire balloting process was a sham, at least in our dorm, and eventually the Communists won with a 90% majority in this bogus election.

* * *

At the Medical School the struggle between Christian or "reactionary" students, as they were labeled, and the new so-called "progressive" Communist opportunists striving for political power, started in the fall of 1947, coinciding with the political showdown in the country. The time-honored Slovak Club of the Medical Students and its democratic majority reelected its president, Ján Štrbák, a senior medical student who was about to graduate, to be their chairman. The Czechoslovakist and Communist faction of students under the leadership of Dušan Brucháč, a radio commentator before coming to the Medical School, organized an opposition group called Oblom. After the "Victorious February" of 1948, Brucháč won and on May 13, 1948, he dissolved the Slovak Medical Club and folded its membership into the Czechoslovak Youth Organization of the Medical School. Štrbák and his group were expelled from the Medical School and later charged with high treason. In a sham trial Štrbák was sentenced to 12 years in jail, where he died laboring in a gulag of uranium mines. The new Communist student body showed its teeth and ruthlessness immediately and presented itself as a formidable and evil force following its own selfish agenda. It was obvious that they did not have a "human face."

In February 1948, the new Communist student avant-garde under the leadership of D. Brucháč, Miloš Brix (who only five years earlier had participated at the leadership meeting of the Slovak Hlinka's Youth organization at Hodruš Lake), V. Zvara, J. Zachar and J. Gero occupied the Dean's office (he had been eliminated by then) and the administration of the Medical School, together with their obedient lackeys and opportunistic associates. The Czechoslovak Youth Organization under this dubious leadership was one of the most politically active and evil organizations at the University.

A series of defining meetings of the student body were called in the auditorium of the University in February 1948 where comrade Brucháč was flanked by the Dean of the Medical School, Dr. H. Krsek, his future father-in-law. Comrade Brucháč, with the help of his henchmen, completed the important political unification of the student body under the banner of his Czechoslovak Youth Organization, in which membership was now compulsory.

The imperative of democratization or cleansing of the student body from its reactionary elements was now vital, following the directive of the General Secretary of the Communist Party, Rudolf Slánský-Salzam: "After the cleansing of the reactionary professors we will mercilessly cleanse the Universities of the reactionary students as well!"[2] The tirades continued: "We need a new system of study dictated by the students and not by the professors with a new relationship to Medical Science based on a strictly materialistic point of view." The political ideology at the school had to be emphasized to support Marxism-Leninism. Every student had to be an integral part of the Czechoslovak Youth Organization. The medical students, with the avant-garde of the assistant professors, had to coordinate their studies and work together with the blue-collar workers of neighboring factories and agricultural cooperatives to learn about their working conditions, physical labor and their zeal for the Communist Party.

The next meeting of this youth organization was held on March 25, 1948, presided over by Mikuláš Toldy, Jozef Szántó and Emil Huraj. They emphasized the importance and the political influence of the medical students at faculty meetings. These student leaders pushed both for concessions in the curriculum and leniency in the rigorous exams for the leading members of the organization, Communists and partisans. Instead of studying hard, it was easier for them to prattle and bully the professors at the faculty meetings. In May 1948 and again on June 1, 1950, Professors of Anatomy Dr. E. Šteklacová was viciously attacked by these Communist cowboys for the rigor of the examinations in human anatomy and, once again, demanded privileges for politically progressive—usually poor—students. Many of these Communist elites passed their exams and advanced in what was a three-year course, or 12 major exams, in a single year.

The whole atmosphere of friendship and collegiality at the Medical School froze during these dramatic events where character assassination menaced everyone except the Communists and their flunkies. Anyone could become a political target and therefore everyone was insecure and frightened, fearing that his day would come soon. A division also developed between the Communists and the apolitical students in our class of 1952. The members of the new elite suddenly changed their behavior: their facial expressions exuded superiority and a new importance. Their heads were held higher, their gaze penetrating, their entire body language projected supremacy over the rest of us at the bottom of the heap. They associated strictly amongst themselves, secretive and scheming in their Communist cells. To gain better control, and a political oversight of the students, the class was broken into smaller groups where each student had to fill out a questionnaire about his family background, social and political

history, class origin, and religious persuasion. Every Catholic was suspected of reactionary convictions or worse, activities.

The first wave of student certifications came in 1949 with the
goal of weeding out the inferior students, nicknamed the "eternals."
And yet, some of the eternals trailing one to three years behind curriculum requirements managed to save their skins by virtue of the
political ties: Ivan Blaho, Miloš Brix, Marta Mrázová, Vladimír
Horný, Jozef Jezerský, Braňo Brozman, and Jozef Šolc, to name just a
few.

In 1950 came the so-called Bolshevik "democratization" or
cleansing. This began in earnest after the Communist students took
over the decision-making process at the faculty meetings, thus turning
themselves into a decisive force in the concerns of the Medical
School.

Simultaneously, political secretaries at the Medical School were
appointed by the Party to keep the school under their political guidance and control. These chieftains kept all the professors and members of the faculty in line, even those who were politically correct.
One of the most noted was Dr. Vladimír Maňák, appointed by the
Central Committee. He later studied communal hygiene in Moscow
and returned with the Soviet degree of Candidate of Science. But
other secretaries excelled as well in those tumultuous times such as
Stanislav Maár, Jozef Kolesár, Jozef Zachar, Pavol Mäsiar, Jozef
Viščor and František Rovňák. In the students' Communist Party, the
secretary was our classmate Stano Dubravicky.

With all political actors in place, the certifying commission could
start its hatchet job. A variation of the same Communist students who
graduated in the years 1948–1951 and our own classmates were our
arbiters. The signatures of D. Brucháč and J. Zachar and others em-
bellish many record books of the democratized and dismissed
students. The criteria for "democratization"—that is, expulsion—from
the Medical School were class origin and the religious and political
background of the student's family, not his failure or shortcomings in
academic requirements. These were political assassinations.

The worst kind of family history consisted of students whose
parents were doctors, lawyers, technical intelligentsia, bankers and
businessmen. Village bourgeoisie with some land—the so-called
"kulaks"—were also a tasty morsel for these investigators. Parents

who were educators, professors and teachers were thoroughly x-rayed for political correctness. The worst liability, however, was membership in the Catholic Church, which was paramount to virtual proof of disloyalty or opposition to the Communist regime. The label of "clerical," that is, religious churchgoer, was the kiss of death for a student. Communist informants, police or civil servants in the student's hometown corroborated the background checks and the information was transformed to the certifying commission at the Medical School. The medical students were then viciously interrogated by these new young Communist doctors. Their work was assisted by informants from our own class who tried to enhance their political standing by bringing in tidbits of gossip and innuendoes as evidence, snooping around during time spent at the school. Our own classmates were many times our worst enemies because they obviously knew a lot about everyone and they could make or break a future career. Especially fiendish and dangerous were the members of the Communist sorority! After intense interrogation and grilling by the commission, the victim had to hand over their "index" or book of school records and they were immediately expelled from the Medical School and their records transferred to the political authorities and civil service for further disposal.

About 200 innocent medical students were dismissed in the early 1950's, almost 20 % of the student body, and some 1000 students were altogether expelled from the University on drummed-up political charges. Only a fraction of them could return after two to five years of doing "other things" to finish their studies. These students were marked for life, getting the worst jobs even as physicians in the backwaters of the country.

The expelled students were not at liberty to do whatever they wished, but were subject to rigorous "reeducation," meaning that they were forcibly assigned to manual labor in coal and uranium mines, stone quarries, and brick factories, among other work sites. They built railroad tracks or toiled in iron foundries or forced labor camps. Others found that "reeducation" meant serving in the military for 2 to 5 years. Some were jailed for many years on fictitious charges for high treason, without recourse to any sort of legal proceeding or defense, and a handful of them died, such as Jozef Štrbák, Albert Pučík, Anton Tunega and Ondreg Vitkovský.

* * *

As part of their political and ideological reeducation, all University students had to participate in manual labor and aid in the massive projects of socialism to demonstrate their loyalty to and appreciation of the Communist system, and to retain the privilege of studying at an institution of higher learning. After finishing my first year at the Medical School, in the spring of 1948,I was assigned to work on the "Railroad of the Youth," a projected rail track between the main rail line and a small but important mining town, Banská Štiavnica, where gold, silver and copper had been produced by German miners since the Middle Ages. It had a famous Mining Academy where the renowned Austrian physicist Christian Doppler had been a teacher in 1847.

Manual labor was nothing new to me. Since losing my beloved father, I had worked as an apprentice bricklayer and did manual labor in construction and road-building in order to support my financially-strapped family. But on June 10, 1948, on my mother's birthday and a week before my final exams in physics, I was unexpectedly struck by an attack of appendicitis and was rushed into surgery. I spent two weeks in the hospital, after which a young resident surgeon left me with a four-inch scar on my abdomen. Of course I missed my exam and presumed, with youthful naivete, that my surgery and the fact that I had been out of commission for weeks, would excuse me from the "brigade," as the labor for the Railroad of the Youth was called. In early September I reported to the dorm, wanting to cram for the physics exam and presented my excuse, a note of surgical discharge. Comrade Ján Jedinák, the Party boss, looked at me with narrowed eyes and burst into a tirade: "What the hell do you think, that this piece of paper should excuse you from building our socialist projects?" I had to go and build student barracks for three weeks to get housing for myself in the dorm for the coming year.

In the summer of 1949, I again packed my rucksack and departed, not knowing what to expect. After a night on the train, a group of us converged from all over the country and arrived at a small railroad station that was the gateway into a picturesque valley—our home for the following four weeks. The students were loaded onto trucks and dispersed into different camps along the valley of the future railroad. I was assigned to camp number 7 where about 150 university students were housed. We arrived at the camp on a warm afternoon, jumped off the trucks and lined up at attention before the members of the General Staff and the Commander-in-Chief. They reviewed us and assessed our physical and spiritual dispositions.

At ease and in line, we were approached by a student in the blue shirt of the Czechoslovak Youth Organization, which was intimately involved in running this show. He approached us with an unfamiliar contraption that looked like a cylinder pump with a piston. Standing out there in the open, we were ordered to loosen our belts and pants. Everyone in line looked uncomfortable, uncertain what to expect. The fellow took this pump, shoved it down our pants in front of everyone and delivered a mighty puff of some kind of powder. Later we learned that it was DDT against lice infestation. Embarrassed chuckles and bursts of artificial giggles followed each puff and breach of privacy, but no one was really amused at this public display.

We were then escorted by our guards to the crude wooden shacks were about 20 students were assigned to live under the same roof. Everyone got a plank bunk padded only with loose straw and a blanket and a burlap straw pillow. A single light bulb lit the entire shack. The sanitary conditions were primitive if not dangerous, with half-covered latrines and a nearby wash area of water pipes with several faucets in the open air where everybody did his best to get clean. The waste was directed into a small brook. It was not surprising that small epidemics, gastrointestinal problems and dysentery developed.

The food was simple and monotonous. In the morning we received black coffee—no milk, but with bromide to keep our hormones in check. In addition, dark bread with margarine or marmalade was given to us. At noon we ate meat, usually pork, with potatoes and a few vegetables, mostly canned or beans. In the evening it was starchy noodles with cheese or dumplings filled with prune butter or the like.

We went to work daily in two shifts, in the morning and afternoon, in small groups where the task was to transfer soil from one place to another on two-wheeled carts or small wagons on rails used in the mines. It was not terribly hard work and since it was summer, the fresh air and beauty of nature made it tolerable. Sometimes we worked in the kitchen peeling potatoes or making and cooking dumplings with marmalade, which was fun. The evenings were dull but we were tired and went to bed early to be ready for the next day's 6 a.m. roll call. The worst part was the weekends, when we were mostly confined to the camp with Saturday morning spent cleaning and sweeping the camp. On Saturday afternoon or Sunday morning compulsory political reeducation was the rule. Occasionally, passes were given to allow us to visit neighboring camps, but going to Sunday church services was unthinkable. The highlight of Saturday evening was a bonfire, songs and cautious camaraderie.

The reeducation lectures were given by instructors from a group of Communist students who were processed through quick training courses since the "Victorious February" of 1948. Most of these instructors had extremely shallow knowledge of the ideology and were only pumped up with empty slogans and political clichés. By raising tricky questions, these lackeys were easy to startle or embarrass. But this was risky and an easy way to get on the blacklist. While we sat on the ground in small circles, an instructor extolled the shining example of the Soviet Union and its struggle for peace. The leading role of the Communist Party was always on the menu with the wise Josef Stalin at the helm. We were taught to be ever-vigilant against the enemies of the people and to be watchful of opportunities to unmask the reactionaries. In our circle we looked at each other and mused, what enemies? But there was a concentrated effort to always discredit the church and religion and it was obvious that they were talking about the Catholic Church and *its* religion as the opiate of the masses. By and large, the lectures were simplistic, dull and anti-intellectual renditions with significant anti-religious underpinnings. I doubt that they changed the view of anyone unless there was a willingness and personal interest to join the in-crowd and the Party.

But not everything was in order during our stay. Some clues gave us a more realistic view of who, exactly, we were working for. As mentioned earlier, even in the midst of summer when vegetables and fruit were plentiful in all of the surrounding villages, they rarely made an appearance in our daily fare. But we noticed that large trucks with food and vegetables left the valley every day. The Headquarters and General Staff were located in the middle of the valley and we knew that the leaders were mostly failed students from the University, flanked by blue-collar Party officials who really ran the show. As we later learned, this Communist elite also had a Communist business ethic: the trucks full of choice fruit and vegetables meant for their socialist projects and the nation's youth were driven across the nearby Hungarian border and the contents sold on the black market through a middleman. He pocketed a significant amount of money from this exchange. Eventually, the whole black market scheme was discovered and broken up, and the leaders of the General Staff were removed, but everything was hushed up and nobody went to jail.

The General Staff and the ringleaders enjoyed other privileges as well. The Chief Health Officer was comrade Skandera, a formerly expelled medical student in his late thirties. To keep the hygienic standards at least at the minimum level and avoid some major health problems—even though we were exposed to some nasty bedbugs—the members of the camp went to the nearby wooden shacks with a heating plant for a weekly hot shower. Everyone was happy to thoroughly wash off a week's worth of sweat and the mood at the showers was merry and mischievous.

There was a girls' camp in the valley as well and they followed the same regimen to maintain their sanitary needs. On one occasion, as a group of female university students was taking their shower, some of them noticed holes drilled into the wooden planks of the shower stall, and worse, eyes behind the holes. The women began to scream and some of them jumped into their shorts and t-shirts while still wet. They were quite upset by this subterfuge and the manner in which comrade Skandera entertained some leering members of the General Staff. The women were outraged at this blatant breach of privacy and filed a vitriolic complaint that resulted in Skandera being sacked and his peep-show discontinued. The women were, of course, not reticent to complain and the whole episode spread through the camps of the valley and thus we students learned about the moral rectitude of the Communist leaders of the General Staff.

The last memorable event happened just about one week before we were ready to leave our labor camp and go home. It was a beautiful summer morning on our last Saturday when we cleaned our barracks and put our bunks in order. Many of us in this camp were from the Svoradov dorm, but other dorms were represented as well as "builders of socialism." A clandestine message came to us by word of mouth that an open-air Mass would be served for the Catholic students in the small neighboring hamlet of Kozelnik at 5 p.m. We were quite overjoyed because many of us were Catholics and for over a month had been unable to attend church services. The small village was about half a mile away and so after 4 p.m., one by one we sneaked out of the camp through the woods, avoiding all roads until we arrived at this tiny community wedged in a ravine. A noticeably larger farmhouse stood in the middle of the cluster of houses. A rather short man with grayish hair and soft blue eyes dressed in a shabby gray overcoat and dirty trousers, looking like a local laborer, stood by talking to a farmer. A small dirt-covered motorbike was at his side. The farmer pointed to the horizontal mantelpiece and the small man started to spread the vestments on the lintel and produced a wooden box for a small chalice. About 50 students who lurked in the background now entered the courtyard, ready for the simple service in this rustic setting. We were, of course, very naive to presume that a Judas would not betray his brethren and report to the masters, the Chief and General Staff of the camp.

Suddenly, from the side road, a pack of young men emerged, headed by a tall, athletic figure easily recognizable to all of us, comrade Tarabčák, the commander of Camp 7. Flanked by a dozen of his goons, all in casual shorts and t-shirts, they broke through the ranks of the surrounding students and made a path for their boss. This robust athlete, aware of his political position and power in the center of this small drama, accosted the small but wiry priest. The commander, a young Communist doctor, was aware that he had no legal right to obstruct the priest's service in a private house, so he relied on the physical power of his gang, which encircled and threatened the priest with a chokehold. One of the men in this pack was a tall, handsome, tanned, would-be medical student. He was the son of a Protestant pastor who came from the heartland of Slovakia. He, like the others, puffed out his chest and flexed his muscles to hinder or abort the service—the same that his own father would serve on the Sabbath.

The commander hollered at the priest and let him know in no uncertain terms that he would not be able to serve the Mass for the students because he and his crew would physically prevent it. For a second, a fleeting smile appeared on the serene face of the churchman, perhaps a thought that this brutish opponent had forgotten the usual outcome in history of the struggle between good and evil. Without a word or glance toward the commander, the priest collected his chalice and vestments. For a second he looked at us as a lost and condemned flock, blessed us all with a brief gesture, jumped on his dirty scooter and disappeared in a cloud of dust. We felt like beaten dogs, while Tarabčák, with a contemptuous sneer on his face, looked upon us as the misguided flock under the influence of the opium of the people. Taking the pastor's son with him, he left together with his pack of wolves at his heels. In the years to come, the pastor's son had a brilliant medical career, passing through the reformed Medical School with flying colors. He was one of the most traveled scientists in Czechoslovakia, visiting not only Western Europe but the United States and Australia as well. As a result, he was attained a great deal of Western knowledge and scientific know-how and therefore climbed with ease to the heights of academia, leaving the less fortunate far behind. There was no contesting his political credentials since he proved his allegiance and abandoned his father's precious heritage.

* * *

At the Medical School the new Communist elite used their Party membership as a springboard for their future careers, even though most of them had joined the Party only in 1948. The Communist ruling class, according to their own desires, went for further training and specialization in Prague to the best institutions and defined the privileged few who could strive for the Soviet title of Candidate of Science. After two or three years of training, they returned to the departments of their choice and were regarded as the best and the brightest in their field. They were treated like gods (Zvara, Brucháč, Turský, Praslička, Mäsiar). Others were handpicked for exclusive positions at the Slovak Academy of Science (Gero, Jansová-Gerová, Zachár, Beliacková-Zacharová).

The other half of this "politically correct" elite, many from my class of 1952, betrayed their youthful idealism to further their careers and got desirable appointments as assistant professors in the specialties of their choice. With the ink on their diplomas still wet—and they themselves still wet behind the ears—they started as the new generation of teachers, usurping the exclusive positions at the Medical School where their political affiliation was their most important leverage. Except for a handful of these Communists, all of those who graduated without major political credentials, no matter how talents, went to work in the countryside.

The primary thrust of the new Soviet ideological influence in medicine was in the biologic sciences, genetics, and the Pavlovian higher neural functions of the brain. Suddenly the teachings of the Soviet peasant agronomist Trofim Lysenko, who had no formal education and who introduced "vernalization" into agriculture (which turned out to be an unmitigated disaster), was taught in our biology class. Since Lysenko rejected the existence of genes, so did our biology professor. He made a complete U-turn from his previous lectures where he taught us about chromosomes and the "crossing-over" of genetic materials. Now "coacervates" and "living matter" were in vogue, the professor failing to demonstrate the physical evidence of these fraudulent theories.

The Pavlovian teachings propounded by the Soviets were now vulgarized in the lectures of pathophysiology by the new assistant professor, Milan Nikš, who had signed up with the Party in 1948. With an appreciable exuberance and arrogance, he harangued us with the self-assurance of an expert in the field for years. A sleepy-eyed, platinum blond Communist vestal flanked him in these paeans to mechanistic science, instructing us that the brain was like a house made up of two floors of upper and lower neural activity. This complex topic was projected with such primitive simplicity that only a fool would buy it. The professor of the department was more circumspect and reticent and stuck to the classical and time-tested evidence in his field. Jansová, the sleepy-eyed blond, pursued her career in Prague and then at the Slovak Academy of Science. Dr. Nikš remained the heir apparent to the Chair in Pathophysiology. He was a rather flamboyant personage, having problems with alcohol, but eventually with his Party badge he made it safely to Lecturer and finally Chairman. His upward path ended rather unceremoniously during a sumptuous lunch when, after a couple of drinks, he suffocated on a piece of food, nobody being able to help him by applying the Heimlich maneuver.

In Medical Physiology the new lecturer, who very quickly sidelined his professor, was a lanky fellow with a neurotic kind of body language and personal arrogance boosted by his pristine Party credentials. He was more ridiculous than outrageous. Braňo Brosman used to come totally unprepared for his lectures, obviously busy with Party politics, but nobody dared to raise a complaint against him. He sat down behind the lectern, opened the textbook and literally read the topic under discussion out of the book. At the end of his lecture, always punctually over on the hour, he shut his book and left. No questions, no discussion. The teaching skills of Ján Kubis, the lecturer in Chemistry, were in the same league, straight out of the chemistry textbook.

The whole curriculum of the lectures was fundamentally changed in the course of a single year by these newcomers, based on a chimerical Soviet model that nobody understood. This was a journey through completely unknown territory led by young political zealots just barely graduated from the Medical School who pretended to have the knowledge of a seasoned expert when theirs was really only skin-deep and without appreciable experience in teaching, let alone research in the field.

In the clinical subjects the influence of the newly politicized group was subtler even though the new secretaries of the "cathedras" were guarding their future domains. The Department of Pediatrics was perhaps an exception since, after the dismissal of Dr. Chura, it suffered through a period of transients until it finally found a keeper: Dr. Jaroslava Michaličková, a Communist luminary, eventually stepped into the fray and inherited the chair. Born in Prague, she studied medicine in Bratislava, where she graduated in 1940 during the interwar Slovak Republic. Serving first as a resident and assistant professor, in 1953 she was nominated as lecturer when she took over the department. Her husband's political standing in the Central Committee of the Communist Party significantly boosted her career, even though she was already known for her left-wing affiliation during Chura's reign. She was smart enough and continued Chura's work in the area of respiratory diseases, but she was not in his league in her professional accomplishments.

To enhance her professional standing, Michaličková initiated a nationwide debate about the proper term for lung infection as if this was the country's most urgent respiratory problem. This was called pneumonia in everyday medical jargon, from the Greek root of *pneumo* = lung. But infection was an inflammatory process and in medicine this usually used the suffix "itis," as in "otitis," the infection of the middle ear. As Michaličková did not like the word pneumonia, she invented a new one by marrying the Greek *pneumo* with the Latin *itis* to come up with "pneumonitis." Of course she became the laughingstock of all pediatricians but no one dared laugh in her face. In her department, "pneumonitis" carried the day.

But there were more important and pressing respiratory problems in the land as a consequence of unchecked industrial pollution caused by the mega-project of socialism in this Communist country. Respiratory problems in children rose to an epidemic level but Michaličková did not attack this national problem as the leading pediatric authority in the land when the political connections of her husband could have been of value in mitigating, if not resolving, this problem. Nothing was done which would slow down the pace of industrialization and the building of socialism.

After Michaličková's retirement, her successor was another devoted Communist assistant professor from the other Department of Pediatrics. She was an extremely mediocre political appointee, who for 19 years as an assistant professor did not have any appreciable professional accomplishments. Facing an unrewarding future with a demanding senior professor in her own department, she transferred loyalties to her political soul-mate, Dr. Michaličková, who took her into the department and pushed her up the academic ladder to the level of full professor. Dr. Anna Randušková ultimately inherited the Chair of the Department of Pediatrics and remained in this leading position even after the fall of Communism in 1991.

*   *   *

The Communist officials knew that, even after the "democratizing" of 200 students from the school, they could not really trust the student body. Therefore, they devised a new scheme where they recruited a group of would-be medical students from factories or cooperatives and anointed them the new proletarian avant-garde. These blue-collar workers in their late twenties, who had never attended high school, were first concentrated in a dorm and in one year crammed with eight years worth of high school and then given their high school diploma *en masse*. They were then accepted into the Medical School without any tests or screening and, as the workers' cadre, processed through in six years. The curriculum had to be adjusted and a great deal of support given to this group and most of them made it through the school. Until this day nobody knows the results regarding the professional outcome of this disastrous experiment which was abandoned shortly thereafter.

From 1950 on, to change the makeup of the medical students and advance the social engineering from another angle, the criteria for acceptance to the Medical School changed drastically. Student excellence and high grades were no longer the primary requirements but rather political allegiance was of paramount importance— enormous advantage was given to the students from a politically correct background. For the mere mortal who intended to study medicine, his high school had to investigate the student's political and class background. The Czechoslovak Youth Organization at the local level had to inform the medical schools of their political criteria. If the student's family background was found to be politically unreliable or even merely lukewarm, the fate of the student was sealed. Any association with the Catholic Church spelled the end of any hope. On the other hand, if the parents were members of the Communist Party or had been a partisan or participant in the resistance or the Slovak National Uprising, the student gained a decided advantage. Therefore, the sons and daughters of blue-collar workers or the proletariat and offspring from agricultural cooperatives were the first contenders. Only after thorough background checks were considered did high school grades become important, but these were definitely *not* decisive factors for admission to the University.

By and large, the offspring of the intelligentsia, especially children of high school teachers, were harshly screened by the new educators of the Communist youth. These parents were spied upon to see if they attended church services; even their own children were prey to entrapment, enticed to betray their own parents. Likewise, the children of physicians, lawyers, businessmen or well-to-do farmers were all potential enemies of the people. Needless to say, in these times of suspicion, distrust and betrayal, many personal accounts were settled where the children ended up as victims of revenge.

As a consequence, many of the brightest students in the country could not attend institutions of higher learning and bore the political burdens of the past and the sins of their parents. A tremendous injustice occurred in this matter in the following 40 years in the name of Communist social engineering.

Despite the initial zeal for this class metamorphosis of the future Communist intelligentsia, from the 1960's on, significant failures and shortcomings in the screening process developed thanks to the human foibles of the apparatchiks as well as the administrators and new medical professionals and professors. These were the ultimate gate-keepers of the admissions process of the University and eventually they succumbed to corruption. For a car and its key, a dacha, or a large sum of money, the officials at the Medical School could find the ways and means around the political barricades and individual students whose parents could provide the "right stuff" were sneaked into its new class. But the vast majority of parents had no such means to overcome this "ideological" obstacle. In the early 1960's an attending physician, Dr. E. M., plucked up her courage and went to see a colleague at the admitting commission to beg him to help her son be admitted to the Medical School. Her classmate and onetime friend gave her a rude awakening and surprised her with a scolding. She should think better than to believe that he would put his neck on the line without a significant bribe. This man was one of many physicians who demonstrated that he was a true believer in Marxist ideology.

Eventually my own sojourn at the Medial School came to an end. In 1947, our class started out as a large one with about 500 students, but after struggling through the rigorous exams in the Basic Sciences, half of the class dropped out. Toward the end, nearing graduation, again a significant number were lost and so about one hundred students of the original class headed for the commencement ceremony. During the final two years, our class of 1952 swelled in size when a last chance was given to the limping along "eternal" students, mostly Party members out to make it or break it, since the new faculty also wanted to close this less honorable chapter. In addition some of the minor political offenders who were dismissed during their democratization were allowed to finish their last year and move on. Thus, over 300 medical students were the lucky ones who dressed up for the final honors and degree.

It is interesting to examine the statistics of the medical graduates of the Medical School in Bratislava and make some comparison with the numbers of graduates in the United States.[3] In the years from 1920 to 1947, between 55 to a high of 85 medical students graduated yearly in Bratislava. In the United States, the number of graduates per medical school in the concurrent years was between 36 and 70 students. From 1948, in Bratislava the number of graduates swelled from 137 (a 65% increase) to 486 (an almost 500% increase) in 1951, and from then on, about 300 medical students graduated annually during the Communist years. In the US during about the same time period, in 1950 there were 70 graduates and in 1994, 124 graduates per school who finished their medical studies. In conclusion, during the four decades beginning with the "victorious" 1948 when Communism was installed, a staggering number of 12,000 medical doctors were produced. One has to wonder if this precipitous increase in the quantity of doctors was necessary and if this increase in quantity was matched by the quality of the graduates during these politically charged years. It seems that medical merit was compromised by the political tenor of the times.

In the last chapter of my medical odyssey, just before graduation, like every student, I had to go before a "distributing commission" to be distributed like a sack of potatoes around the country, with no questions asked and no choices given. Here again, for the last time, we were profiled to see if we could serve the people in the "people's democracy" of our state. We were eventually asked what we would like to do, what specialty we were interested in and in which part of the country we would like to serve. It was, of course, a political charade for the naive and the authorities really did not care where we went or what we wanted to do if we were not part of the Communist elite. The Communists, instead of setting an example and pioneering their ideology in the country towards the people with the greatest medical needs, secured choice placements for themselves in the capital and in various departments of the Medical School or at the Slovak Academy of Science. Regarding the rest of our class, no matter how brilliant a student was, he or she was assigned to a remote county or district hospital where career opportunities were limited and the possibility of making a U-turn to get back to the Medical School was rather small. It was obvious that everybody of sound mind and ambition wanted to remain in the capital or close by because there was a tremendous medical-technological and professional gap between the opportunities in the capital or in the western part of the country versus 300 miles eastward facing the border with the Soviet Union.

One by one, we went before this commission, which was chaired by the noted Vladimír Zvara, a graduate from two years back, Jozef Jerzerský, and other political movers who were flanked by our own Communist classmates—these were the people who would decide our fate and future. This was the unbelievable reality! Any chance to be placed according to our grades or achievements at the Medical School was out of the question. Choice of placement was only a mirage. We were herded before this political tribune to get what we deserved, according to them.

There were some outstanding students in our class from the non-Communist group, indeed the best brains of the class who deserved to stay at the Medical School based on their excellence and desire to serve medical science. One of these was a brilliant student, B. V., a potbellied, bespectacled blond "professor" from our dorm—a bright and happy fellow with a voracious appetite and a fantastic chess player blessed with a bristling wit. His parents were emigrants who fled the Russian Revolution of 1917, being of "white" (as opposed to "red") Russian background. He was, therefore, destined to be assigned to the eastern-most boundaries of the country to a small rural hospital where he had no chance of doing any research, but to become instead a country G.P. This was how the Communists cared for the intellectual potential of the best youth in the land. His case was not exception but mostly the rule. Many of the superior students were deliberately sent to eastern Slovakia to eliminate possible contenders to sought-after positions in the capital. A group of my friends whose roots were in Bratislava, the so-called "city bourgeoisie," all got their marching orders to the eastern-most part of the country and only a few would make it back to the capital after paying their dues by working five to ten years in the countryside.

In early December 1952, our class graduated in the festive graduation hall at the University. My mother and nuclear family and all the proud parents gathered with bouquets and gifts to congratulate their successful sons and daughters for their hard-won and well-earned diplomas. My financially strapped family knew that it had been taxing for me to go through the years of medical school on a very skimpy budget, with one pair of pants and one green jacket of wartime material that shed green dandruff. As for my black suit for the graduation ceremonies, my tailor had made miracles to alter my dear father's tuxedo to fit me, since my father had been ten inches shorter and the sleeves and slacks had to be extended by craft and stealth to be presentable. A present of fancy black shoes came at the last minute, saving my sartorial integrity to complement my attire, but the shoes were too tight and I had to walk as if on eggshells so as not to slip before the Dean and Rector while receiving my diploma.

The day was really jubilant but we were well aware that under our "makeup," all of us—with our politically suspect or politically dissenting backgrounds, with religious affiliations, and with the ultimate liability of being members of the Svoradov dorm—were looking ahead to a very murky, risky future.

Soon came Christmas and with excitement and rather optimistic naivete, I expected my placement documents, satisfied that I would able to do internal medicine and adult cardiology, as I had fallen in love with electrocardiography and was well versed in it from the reading the seminal textbook in the country. I was assigned to start my internship at the county hospital in Ružomberok, in the heartland of Slovakia.

In the first days of January, 1953, an envelope arrived with the announcement: "With this administrative order by the Ministry of Health, you are obligated to report to the Department of Communal Hygiene in the eastern town of Košice and immediately report to service." I was completely devastated and, together with my family, could not believe this news. I was then, and still am, convinced that this was an act of political retribution and punishment—I was to be professionally sidelined if not destroyed as a consequence of my political passivity. I was not convinced of the righteousness of Marxist-Leninist theory, of dialectic materialism, and of atheism, not only because the theory sounded like a fallacious teaching but also because of the type of people who represented this new fakery, speaking in the name of the "people" and the Communist Party, but acting in their own interests and creating a milieu permeated with lies, deceit, shams and illegal acts. Those of us who questioned their theory and searched for reason and truth had to be destroyed—by our own colleagues, no less—or at least be made into docile second-class citizens. They were the informants and arbiters who were to pass judgment on us, following the Marxist dictates, and were themselves exonerated for all wrongdoing in the name of the Party, while in reality only advancing their own interests. Overnight a small, politically correct group rose to high posts to articulate the political programs. With an appalling lack of professional experience and hardly any other accomplishments, but with revolutionary slogans on their lips, they molded the new medical curriculum into a watered-down version of the Soviet model at the Medical School.

According to my marching orders, instead of training in internal medicine I was now supposed to practice communal hygiene. That is, I was to inspect the water supply and quality of wells and pipes, chlorinate water and waste, and inspect garbage dumps—activities which I had few ideas about and most of all, absolutely no desire to perform. I fell into a deep depression as a consequence of this treachery by the political potentates at the Medical School. Throughout the month of January I was distraught and mentally paralyzed. My dear mother could no longer look at me, huddled in my dad's easychair, staring into space, unaware of my surroundings and leaving her culinary masterpieces untouched. She turned out to be the most resilient warrior, seeking connections and attempting to move mountains to find the right loopholes to extricate me from this bind. She even traveled to the capital and the Ministry of Health to save me from my fate. After many interventions and my own trip to the capital, somebody (bless his soul!) had mercy on me and changed my assignment. Later, I learned that about 15-20 percent of my class was trapped into working in communal hygiene and only one or two were able to wrest free from this destiny and go on to do real medicine.

It was March 1953 when my fortune changed after being on strike for three months. I could have been prosecuted and thrown in jail for disobeying the government's assignment. At this late date, all the places for residents in the Department for Internal Medicine were filled and, as a last resort, I accepted an internship in the Department of Pediatrics, which was the closest related field. I did not know then that this switch was just a harbinger of the ultimate wisdom of Providence and that eventually I would practice electrocardiography on children with congenital heart disease, eventually specializing in pediatric cardiology, which I was never to regret. As a specialist and the first Board-certified pediatric cardiologist in the country, I eventually returned to the Medical School by invitation. After years of hard work and research, my miraculous journey catapulted me to the Promised Land of medical science, the land of my hero, Martin Arrowsmith—the United States of America.

5

The Eastern Massacre

While the historical chronicles of the year 1230 A.D. refer to this eastern metropolis as Košice in the area of geographic Slovakia, its Latin name—Cassovia—suggests perhaps earlier origins. In the Middle Ages the surrounding geographic area was labeled "Partes superiores" or Upperland (as opposed to the Lowlands of southern Hungary proper) and during the Hungarian reign of the town, declared free by the king, it was called Kassa (Kascha)[1].

The town had a rich history and was well managed with its own central administration within the province; it had a mint and a military court as well. In 1369 its population was greater than that of Bratislava, which was to the west, and as one of the leading towns of the Hungarian Kingdom, it had its own crest. In the Middle Ages the city was an important commercial center, being at the crossroads of the north-south axis of Krakow–Budapest–Istanbul, and was an important bastion in the Turkish wars of the 16th and 17th centuries. From the 17th century the town, with the eastern-most university in Europe, became a center of higher education to which the University of Buda(Pest) and the Theological College from Eger (northern Hungary) were transferred during the Turkish wars.[2]

It was here, in 1657, on the initiative of Bishop Kishdy and with the approval of King Ferdinand III, that a university was founded for studies in theology and philosophy.[3] In 1772, the state took over the university and Empress Maria Theresa initiated the establishment of the School of Medicine. This was later turned into a branch of the University of Buda(Pest) with the addition of the School of Law and Philosophy.[4] In 1848, the university underwent another metamorphosis, when it was changed into an Academy for Law and Philosophy, which was closed after 70 years of instruction in 1921 by the central government of Prague, Czecho-Slovakia, as a superfluous education center for the "less educated" Slovak brethren.[5] At this point, the name of Košice was bestowed on the town.

My birthplace, a town of considerable beauty and charm, was settled in a valley straddling a sluggish river surrounded by lovely scenery with forests, hills, and meadows. The crown jewel of the town, the Gothic Cathedral of Saint Elisabeth, has a magnificent altar as its centerpiece and in its crypt, the Hungarian freedom-fighter Prince Francis Rakoczy is buried. St. Michael's chapel, and the nearby ornate and graceful Renaissance theater from the 19th century, is situated in the central square, surrounded by clusters of fountains. This central square, embraced on parallel sides by the silhouettes of beautiful and colorful Renaissance and Baroque palaces as well as the old town hall, is also adorned by churches of different styles, orders and denominations. In the nearby park a stunning Jewish temple, with its monumental cupola and neighboring school, stands slightly off the center like a sleeping beauty. This melange of different churches reflected well on the cosmopolitan nature of the city with its different religions and nationalities, which in the 1930's comfortably and quite tolerantly coexisted. Similar to Bratislava at the turn of the century, this was a mostly Hungarian and German town with the addition of Slovak and later Czech minorities who moved in when in Czecho-Slovakia was established after 1918. These newcomers lived all over the town, but were mostly concentrated in a district called "Little Prague" where, by and large, mutual respect and tolerance was the rule. Having a Catholic majority, the town was also the bishop's seat of the diocese, but there were also a rather significant Lutheran and Calvinist population and a rather strong Jewish constituency with its rabbis and clergy. At the birth of Czechoslovakia, the majority of citizens were trilingual, speaking Hungarian, German and Slovak, especially the older generation.

Until my departure for the Medical School, my youth was spent here, living comfortably and peacefully as part of this mosaic of nationalities and religions. At first glance, commerce on the fashionable main street appeared to be a Jewish domain. My mother shopped for her textiles at Klein & Offner, purchased shoes for the family at Zopf and Faragó, and other items at the department store owned by the Schoenfelds. Mr. Vitez offered his stationery on the northern side of the street while Mr. Gotterer offered his on the southern end. I traded stamps with Mr. Gyuerk and his wife. Besides the groceries from a nearby "consum," where different deli specialties were available, the cheese my mother chose to buy was from Mr. Berger's cellar—he always offered me a snippet of emmental. For the holidays and especially at Christmas, together with my father we visited the wine cellar of Mr. Strauss, whose son Emerich was a classmate of mine. My father used to talk politics with Mr. Weiss, a grocer on the corner, when coming home from his office while he stopped to pick up choice pastries at the Megay's. My pediatrician, the bespectacled and kind Dr. Melchner, watched over my health, checking for rickets and pneumonia while Dr. Friedman took care of my dad's hypertension and the rest of the family.

After the Munich Agreement of September 1938, everything in the town changed as nationalistic pressures were foisted upon all. Later, after the Vienna arbitration in 1939, the town and territory were shunted to Hungary with Hitler's approval. From then on, a general decline in people's relationships and in the atmosphere of the town occurred, especially when the Second World War broke out. In my school, my classmates were either tagged with yellow stars or suddenly disappeared. The targeted Jewish population went into hiding, some into the countryside, but mostly to Budapest. They were deported by the Hungarian authorities to concentration camps. As the war came to an end, the victorious Red Army overran the city, deporting its intelligentsia, priests and "capitalists" in droves without any legal proceedings—these unfortunates were never seen again.

Slowly but surely, survivors of the war—the young soldiers and those from the concentration camps—came out of hiding and returned to the town of their roots, finally claiming their territory and lost possessions. Most of those who had survived this terrible ordeal had been liberated by the Red Army in camps in Poland.

At this tumultuous juncture, when freedom was seen coming from the east and the political order was being significantly bolstered by the Soviet-supported Communist Party, many people joined the Party. This was especially true among educated people. Joining seemed part of an ideological backlash at that time and later, an opportunity to be part of the ruling Communist strata, especially after the Communist coup of February 1948.

It was the Minister of Education, Ladislav Novomeský, who initiated the establishment of a branch of the Medical School in this eastern metropolis during the years 1948/49. It seems that the Minister and his political and medical advisors, carried away by their political zeal, failed to recall history and the experience of the difficult birth of the Medical School in Bratislava. This move was a political decision based on the "divine enlightenment" of the IXth Congress of the Communist Party and by request of its General Secretary and President of the Republic, Klement Gottwald who, as a carpenter trained in Vienna, yearned for a new intelligentsia with roots in the working class.[6]

Insufficient time was allowed to carefully work out a plan for the physical plant for the institution and to set up its personnel and administration because the Communist Party wanted instantaneous results. However, their *modus operandi* placed the cart before the horse. Similar to the situation of the Medical School almost thirty years earlier in Bratislava, the hospital base in Košice was in rather good condition for the clinical semesters, since the main hospital with its system of pavilions for different clinical disciplines could serve a teaching purpose. A great advantage at this time was that a second tier of young professors or lecturers of Slovak origin, with solid experience in teaching, research and administration from the University of Bratislava, already existed. This enthusiastic group provided a promising faculty for the clinical and preclinical departments and, from this point of view, the academic year could be started with the official opening of the Medical School in January 1949. Since the physical plant and structures for the Basic Sciences were not available right away, at first only the clinical semesters were launched.[7]

For these departments the local medical-professional base was only able to provide three department heads since the Surgeon-in-Chief, already a well-established professor and the most qualified teacher, had been appointed as Dean of the Medical School. The other two large departments of Internal Medicine and Pediatrics were already following in the spirit of the times in 1948/49 with political appointments as rewards for previously persecuted physicians.

Dr. František Pór (Pollatschik) (1899–1980) who had studied medicine after 1918 in Budapest and Göttingen and graduated in Prague in 1926, led the Department of Internal Medicine in 1945.[8]

After his graduation he spent six years in Prague at the Department of Internal Medicine at the German branch of Charles IV University, first as a resident and then as an assistant professor. In 1932 he was appointed as the head of the Department of Internal Medicine in a rather small district hospital in the town of Ružomberok, where no academic medicine, teaching or research could be done. During the Slovak Republic he was able to work only as an internist in a smaller town and towards the end of the Second World War, he was sent to the concentration camp at Terezin.[9] From 1945 he was a member of the Communist Party and led the Department of Internal Medicine. In 1950 he was appointed as a state lecturer by the authorities. Pór was not obliged by the Medical School to present a dissertation, as had been required before the Communists came to power. And yet he was an able sage and surrounded himself with an enthusiastic and aspiring younger generation of physicians for who, together with his association with the political authorities and his own adroit skills, he could provide ample encouragement, professional latitude and a scientific environment which consequently fostered a respectable school of followers in the years ahead.

Ferdinand Démant (1911–1985), born in Budapest, became the Chairman of the large Children's Hospital. He studied at the Medical School of Charles IV University in Prague in the years 1929–35, and joined the Communist Party in 1933. After graduation he worked as a resident in Pediatrics at the Children's Hospital in Prague until 1939 at which point the Germans occupied Bohemia and closed the Medical School. Afterwards, in 1940, he appeared, jobless, in Slovakia. From 1941 he worked in a small spa in western Slovakia where he was protected and ultimately saved from deportation and the concentration camps.[10]

In 1945, when the first political cleansings of the faculty began at the Medical School in Bratislava, and the noted Chairman of the Department of Pediatrics there was dismissed, Démant, a rather inexperienced man in academic medicine, had the chutzpah to apply for this position. As pointed out by the Minister of Education, despite his membership in the Communist Party, Démant's lack of experience in teaching, research and academic medicine could not match his political credentials and his appointment was denied.

Fortunately for Démant, there was another large Children's Hospital in the eastern city of Košice. With the help of the Party, he muscled his way through this appointment as a state lecturer without presenting a dissertation. When the Medical School was launched in 1949, Démant was in charge and he inherited the hospital, now a center of medical education, and thus the professorship fell into his lap. He was a mediocre physician and a poor teacher with a total lack of research experience who tried to emulate Dr. Pór's example, but without success. His rounds resembled the catwalk of a fashion show, with very brief presentations or reviews, and with complete lack of any instruction or meaningful discussion. He almost never examined or touched a patient or showed any example of his know-how because his primary concern was his political duties. Démant served as Dean in the years 1950–53 only because he was a Communist big-shot at the Medical School during these politically charged times. He marked the lives of many doctors and students alike during the political cleansings and demonstrations after 1948 when the Communist Party and its members were the defining and determining factors in higher education and, indeed, in every segment of public life. He remained a lifelong member of the Communist Party to which he was thankful for his career and whose orders he dutifully carried out. He did not develop any following of his own because there was nothing to follow.

In the second academic year of 1949/50, the lectures in the basic sciences had to commence according to the marching orders of the Party. They city had to allocate physical plant and buildings for the administration of the Medical School and for the different departments in basic sciences. A large, ornate building previously belonging to the Superior Court was made available to the Dean and the administration.[11]

All the department heads of the basic sciences were young assistant professors from Bratislava. This was a very professional group made up of young, progressive teachers with solid research backgrounds.[12] All of them had to start from scratch because no formal plans or organized preparations had been made ahead of time by their alma mater. At first only limited technology and rudimentary machines and instruments were provided. These were already highly politicized times when medical science was being invaded by ideology which marked the lives of all of these young men in their thirties.[13] The oldest, Professor Dr. J. Skotnický, had been dismissed from the Medical School in Bratislava in 1945 but was now dusted off and appointed as Head of the Department of Medical Physics. The able Dr. Vladimír Munka and Dr. Jozef Zemanik chaired the Departments of Anatomy and Physiology, while the Department of Chemistry was led by Dr. Anton Neuwirth. Dr. Ivan Porazik was appointed to the Department of Histology and Microscopic Anatomy.

The Department of Biology lacked a chairman and was, therefore, supplemented for a year by a biologist, Dr. Jozef Hovorka, from the School of Veterinary Medicine. The field of biology was in peril during these ideologically-charged times, as Soviet biology, with its underpinnings of Dialectic Materialism, was battering down the door of classical cellular biology and its theory of creation and the origins of life. It was, therefore, important for the Communist Party to find the right man who would put into practice the foundations of politically correct biology and establish, once and for all, the undisputed primacy of Soviet biology and related sciences at this medical school.

This task fell on Dr. Anton Millár (1915–), assistant professor from the Department of Internal Medicine. He was the scion of an affluent Jewish family who attended Medical School in Prague, from which he graduated in 1941. He was a survivor of the Auschwitz concentration camp where he had worked as camp physician, helping the suffering and saving lives.[14]

In order to refocus his interest in biology, Millár was sent to the renowned Professor Hercik who taught this science in the Moravian city of Brno where the Benedictine monk, Gregor Mendel, had laid down the fundamentals of modern genetics. After his relatively short training, Millár returned to the Medical School and inherited the chair in Biology and was appointed chairman of the all the basic sciences. Millár, a tall, lanky man with red curly hair and steel-blue bespectacled eyes, gave the impression of being a highly intelligent person, but very soon it became obvious that he was a formidable zealot who, exuding great passion, had a mission to root out everything "reactionary" from the science of biology and medicine. He wanted not only to eradicate classical biology, but also to replace it with a new, revolutionary, materialistic, ideologically atheistic, politicized science. Millár radicalized his zeal into an ideological attack, eliminating a science based on evidence and independent confirmation and replacing it with a bogus discipline supported not by independent investigation but rather by Soviet-provided fraud or forgery.[15] In addition to this goal, he proclaimed a holy war against anyone who did not share his convictions and demanded that such a person provide scientific evidence for his contrary views, a task which could not be achieved at the Medical School without the assistance of the Communist Party and its members there.

The Communist Party at the Medical School was an interesting mixture of Jewish and non-Jewish members. In the early years, the formerly persecuted and harshly tried Jewish members claimed a leading role. The non-Jewish members were mostly novices with former partisan or Czechoslovak dispositions who jumped on the Communist bandwagon, either for self-serving reasons or because they were smitten by the ideological slogans. Thus, Millár had significant support from doctors at the Medical School such as comrades F. Démant, F. Pór, Ladislav and Gerda Bárdoš, Ladislav Meyer, Alexander Gordon, Ladislav Sobel, Jozef Sonderlich (who allegedly was a quisling), Wiliam Grybovský, Magda Sebastianová, Agnes Valková and Peter Hoffman. In the other group, the main actors were Alexander Puza, Ján Ondik, Konštantín Barna, Imrich Ivančo, Andrej Nicák, Daniel Zubrík, and the shady Dean Lukáči, Rudolf Korec, Emil Matejček, Ján Trebula, Michal Pichanič, Vojtech Tischler, Ján Jacina, Olga Pavkočeková, Július Uhrík and the members of the Department for Marxism-Leninism. This strained balance collapsed in 1952 after the anti-Zionist witch-hunt in which the second group prevailed. Under the leadership of Millár and his Communist lackeys, the careers and personal lives of two promising scientists who were appointed to head the Departments of Medical Chemistry and Microscopic Anatomy were doomed.

I met Dr. Ivan Porazik (1923–1996) for the time as a medical student in 1948 when he swooped into the lecture room of the Medical School (Fig. 5.1). He projected a strikingly dramatic personality. At 6'2", with the wide shoulders of an athlete, he had the prominent skull and occiput of a scientist. His high forehead was delineated by prominent eyebrows and bespectacled, inquisitive dark blue eyes, which exuded a self-confidence that was accentuated by his well-articulated and sensuous mouth and well-defined jaw. He was an impressive figure with the disposition of a man who was not shy of being noticed.

He was already considered distinguished at the time of his *magna cum laude* graduation in 1948. Soon after his appointment as assistant professor, he lectured with clarity of mind and also demonstrated that he had done his homework.

In 1950, as the crème de la crème of the young scientists, Porazik was selected by Dean Krsek and the Minister of Education himself, Novomeský, to lead the Department of Microscopic Anatomy at the new branch of the Medical School in Košiče. With the help of Professor Dr. Ivan Stanek from Bratislava, who highly esteemed Dr. Porazik, the Department was founded virtually from scratch. In these dangerous and politically explosive times, Stanek advised Porazik to keep his mouth shut in political matters.

In only a few years, Porazik, with a group of young and enthusiastic associates, presented some original research on the neural supply of the gut and pancreatic isles. However, these remarkable results and his talents as an excellent teacher were not sufficient in the face of the requirements and expectations of the times when medical science was invaded by political ideology and forced to be subservient to it. Here Porazik ran into serious trouble with Dr. Millár, chief biologist and ideologue, who now chaired and oversaw all the departments of the Basic Sciences.

The conflict that developed was not about biology, but rather ideology. According to Millár, it was ridiculous to dwell on the vitalistic or idealistic tenets of the cellular origins of life. "Today," he proclaimed, "everyone knows that life originates from amorphous living matter that generates cells, according to the findings of Soviet scientist Olga B. Lepeshinskaja, a pupil of Trofim Lysenko and I.V. Michurin." The time-honored evidence of Rudolph Wirchov and other Western scientists regarding cellular theory were to be discarded as reactionary. Millár never gave data in support of his statements, but insisted that only the Marxist point of view in biology was scientifically sound. It was of the utmost importance that the teachers of higher education present this "politically correct" view, buttressed by the class-consciousness of the times. The class origins of the members of the Medical School had to be examined, he warned, in order to learn who thought otherwise. He continued: "We will vigilantly examine everyone's work and discover the ideological and class enemies, the political reactionaries." At this time any religious inference or association was the kiss of death. Millár's goal was to wed out the un-reliable or non-conformist individuals and destroy them as political enemies.[16]

Porazik was up against a formidable ideological enemy. In addition to his middle-class origins, he had also spent the summer of 1946 in France, in a Catholic youth organization. The product of a classical medical education, he felt uncomfortable with the new theories and looked for evidence regarding O. B. Lepeshinskaja's medical and scientific record.

Jakov Rappaport, a noted Russian pathologist, summarized her personality and research in 1988. O. B. Lepeshinskaja (1871–1963), a scientist relegated to oblivion in today's Russia, was first a revolutionary with her husband, a contemporary of Lenin's. During their exile in Geneva, the couple ran a Russian tavern. As an "authority" in biology, Lepeshinskaja was trained as a midwife in 1897 in St. Petersburg. In 1906 she graduated as a "feldsher," never having attended a classical medical school. She was a general practitioner for over ten years for railroad workers and, in 1936, with this "scientific" background, she entered the Soviet Institute of Experimental Medicine in Moscow. In 1941 she was head of the department for "Living Matter" at the Institute of Biology at the Soviet Academy of Sciences. As Rappaport chronicles, she was a pugnacious and opinionated woman who worked in a makeshift laboratory with unsophisticated methods and technology for the "basic" research in which she participated.[17]

Lepeshinskaja claimed that amorphous "living matter," as opposed to cells, was the quintessential vehicle of life, thus trying to discredit the cellular genetic evidence of Gregor Mendel and J. Morgan, professor at Columbia University in New York. Despite her volume of research dedicated to Joseph Stalin, her evidence for this theory—if she ever had any—never gained wide acceptance and was severely criticized as artifacts or technical forgery by the biologist D. S. Nasonov.[18] The only support she received was from the Rasputin of Russian biology, T. Lysenko, and academician J. V. Davidovsky, both of whom were interested in serving Stalin and not medical science, thus demonstrating total ethical failure and dishonesty in order to please this barbarian.[19]

Even though Porazik presented this "living matter" theory about the origins of life in his lectures, he remained reserved about it. He let the students make up their own minds. The students sensed his misgivings from his body language and facial expressions and some of them had no qualms about reporting him to Millár.

"It seems that perhaps O. B. Lepeshinskaja's results should be repeated and confirmed by independent experiments," he mused. His doubts regarding her results as a top Soviet scientist were considered highly sacrilegious. Porazik also maintained his longstanding friendship with Dr. A. Neuwirth, and occasionally met on social grounds and informally with Catholic theologians. All of this boded ill for Porazik.

In the 1952/53 academic year, Porazik's ideological résumé or assessment as a "cadre"—a euphemism for his political profile—could not have been worse. Labeled as "bourgeois" because of his origins, he carried significant religious baggage. He respected only the research of western science and was critical of the grandiose Soviet achievements in biology, such as the work of O. B. Lepeshinskaja. Politically and ideologically regarded at a very low level, not a member of mass organizations such as the Communist Party, and without positive relationship to the "people's democracy" or its class struggle, Porazik was, therefore, labeled an unreliable reactionary and an enemy of the Communist Party and the people.

On the very same professional scene at the Košiče Medical School, the drama of his friend, Dr. Anton Neuwirth, also unraveled (Fig. 5.2). Only a year older, Neuwirth graduated from the Medical School in 1947 with stellar credentials. During his studies at the Medical School in Bratislava he lived in the Catholic dorm Svoradov for five years, receiving a religious imprint for life. He enrolled for two additional semesters at the School of Natural Sciences because of his interest in chemistry. Neuwirth, who taught medical chemistry, was compared to Porazik as a peaceful man and a very kind-hearted person. His pleasant demeanor and poise disguised a man of conviction and resolve, as well as his spiritual strength, rooted in deep religious beliefs. After his graduation from the Medical School, he was invited to join the Department of Chemistry as an assistant professor to the towering chemistry professor Dr. F. Valentín. He spent the following year at the Technical High School in Zurich with Nobel laureate Dr. P. Karver.

While working there, Neuwirth also met the American scientist, Dr. Linus Pauling, also a Nobel laureate. Neuwirth made a presentation at a meeting in the presence of Pauling that was later published in *Helvetica Medica Arta*—an achievement that would haunt him and eventually prove to be his downfall.

In late 1948, his superior, Dr. F. Valentín, was dismissed from the Medical School and Neuwirth parted with him with great sadness. The Communist Dean Krsek offered the chair to Neuwirth, but the "politically correct" Ján Kubis prevailed with his Party credentials, even though he had never taught chemistry at any university. Neuwirth vented his misgivings to Dean Krsek before his departure to lay the foundations of the Department of Chemistry at the new Medical School in Kosiče. On leaving, he remarked, "During these ideologically-charged times with the heightened political struggle for Communists to prevail, I am very concerned that I can get into fundamental controversies; and by the way I am not convinced of the correctness of the social theory of Marxism-Leninism." These admissions, which undoubtedly were filed in his political dossier, were fatal mistakes for a young scientist.

In 1949 it was an arduous task to create a Department of Chemistry from virtually thin air, especially when Neuwirth's superior in Bratislava, Dr. J. Kubis, gave little support and only obsolete machines and instrumentation were available for this department. Still, step by step, with a lot of hard work, the help of young associates, and unwavering determination, in three years a fully functional department was born, coupled with excellent teaching, respectable research and some publications as well.

But from the beginning dark clouds gathered over Neuwirth's head. His stance as head of the Department who did not subscribe to the new ideology of Marxism-Leninism as part of his scientific oeuvre made him a target. In his lectures Neuwirth digressed and referred to his research done in Switzerland, which was in accordance with Pauling's theory and findings. But his associate chemist, Daniel Zubrík, took a distorted view of his presentation and reported it the Central Committee of the Communist Party. Zubrík indicated that Neuwirth was teaching the students reactionary theories in contradiction to the Soviet teachings at the time, which attacked Pauling's research.

Fig. 5.1: Dr. Ivan Porazik, 1949

Fig. 5.2: Dr. Anton Neuwirth, 1949

The beginning of the end for Neuwirth was his confrontation with the noted "red biologist," A. Millár; his religious affiliation and convictions only added to his troubles. At the meetings of the Chair, Millár pressed his zealous ideology for Basic Sciences from the Soviet view of "living matter as a cell-free substance," pointing to the egg yolk as an example. This received a sharp retort from Neuwirth that, according to his knowledge, the egg yolk was full of germinating cells and only became cell-free after it was boiled. It was a slap in Millár's face, revealing a fundamental flaw in his biological knowledge.

As a consequence of this tussle, Neuwirth was labeled a reactionary anti-Marxist and was surrounded by a passel of young Communist informers. Even his office was bugged, as he learned when he once surprised a secret agent "repairing" his telephone. The final straw that sealed Neuwirth's fate was that he was a deeply religious person. Even though he avoided any reference to it in his professional conduct, he was a practicing Catholic even in those times of vicious anti-Catholic and anti-Church sentiment. He and some other colleagues used to have informal social meetings within a lay organization called "the Family," advocating lifelong commitment to the teachings of Jesus Christ. Naturally, some clergymen and theologians joined in, namely the distinguished Dr. Jozef Jenčik. Jenčik was the principal target of the Communist Party, since his Sunday sermons in the Cathedral attracted the youth of the entire city. When it came to fundamental matters and principles of his faith, Neuwirth stood fast. He was the proverbial iron fist in a velvet glove. When a letter was circulated at the Medical School asking faculty to condemn the Catholic bishops of Slovakia (who were all soon to be incarcerated), he refused to sign it. The Dean of the Medical School, Dr. F. Démant, accused him of being an enemy of the state and threatened him with grave punishment.

Eventually Neuwirth's noncompliance in professional and private matters came to a head and it was only a question of time before the Communist Party, under the leadership of Millár and his comrades, would strike. In the meantime, Linus Pauling received the Nobel Peace Prize because he proposed the banning of all nuclear weapons, and the Soviets awarded him with the Stalin Prize. After that they accepted all of Pauling's previously rejected theories in molecular chemistry. It was, however, too late for Neuwirth.

On November 30, 1953, three unidentified men kidnapped Dr. Porazik as he was walking home for lunch, in broad daylight near the Greek Orthodox church. They pushed him into a car, sandwiched him between two agents, blindfolded him and drove him nearly non-stop through the night, without food or water, over 500 miles to Prague. At this time Porazik was thirty years old, with a young wife and a nine-month-old son. He was transferred to the infamous Ruzyňe prison, stripped naked, photographed and fingerprinted. A striped prison outfit with a cap, mess tin, a spoon and two blankets which stank of disinfectant were his sole possessions. For a year he was left in solitary confinement like a hardcore criminal, in a cubicle with only a bunk and bucket for waste. For sixteen hours a day he walked five steps forwards and backwards in maddening desperation—why had this happened? He lost 70 pounds, and at the time of his sentencing one year later, this 6'2" skeleton weighed 110 pounds.[20]

In October of 1954, as if in a Golgothean scene, in the presence of his beloved wife and mother, whom he was seeing for the first time since his kidnapping, Porazik was sentenced. If they had not called his name, his wife would not have recognized him for he had changed so much. He was charged with high treason and espionage against the people's democracy and the working class. There was no jury, just three state judges—Jaroslav Novák, Ondrej Grznár, and Tomáš Kuracina—and a court appointed defense in cahoots with the government. The prosecutor asked for the death sentence. Porazik received a sentence of eleven years in jail without parole. It was later learned that the charge was based on three anonymous letters received from his own colleagues at his Medical School, later revealed to have been written by Dr. Andrej Millár, Daniel Zubrík, an assistant professor (now allegedly in the United States), and a Dr. K., whose name remains a mystery, and is probably a cover anyway.[21]

"Prisoner No. 851 reports in attention," was the formula and rule when Porazik was repeatedly interrogated. Increasing the psychological pressure, the commander of the prison yelled at Porazik: "You have to come to terms with yourself and admit your treason." When Porazik tried to reason with his tormentors, that he did not know what they were talking about, they ridiculed him. His failure to shows signs of reeducation, redemption or remorse only made his situation worse.

Meanwhile, his wife was expelled from the Medical School just before her graduation and was forced to earn her living as a nurse's aid. In despair, she went to see the Associate Dean, the shady Dr. Jozef Lukáči, pleading for help. He assured her: "Our justice system is fair! If your husband is innocent, he will be released. If, on the other hand, he is guilty, he will receive a fair punishment." As he was known for being hand-in-glove with the police, Lukáči knew very well that Porazik was considered to be guilty.[22]

Incarcerated at the uranium mines of Jáchymov, which now worked exclusively for the Soviets, after some training Porazik worked as the anesthesiologist in the makeshift hospital of the prison camp. He soon realized that within the camp he was amid a congregation of intellectuals from the entire country. He met Jewish Communist intellectuals who were sent there after the Zionist purges of 1952—men such as Arthur London, Deputy Minister of the Interior, who was very ill with tuberculosis, and Edward Goldstücker, the writer, whose face was that of a suffering saint. Judged as class enemies, many physicians were also there, such as Professor Dr. Karel Koch from Bratislava and Dr. Eichler, and many others. The brave Czech airmen who had flown in the Royal Air Force and had fought against Hitler and, in counterpoint, the now discredited Communist fighters of the Spanish Civil War, were present as well. A dazzling mixture of reputable people were held as political prisoners. Two hundred Catholic priests, mostly from Slovakia, were held in this "camp of death," mining the uranium for the Soviets without any protection against radioactivity. Many medical students from the 1948 purges were here as well, including the chairman of their Medical Students Club, Andrej Štrbák, who eventually could not take the torture and died. Other students followed him to their deaths, like Albert Pučík, Anton Tunega, Ondrej Vitkovský and Imrich Jánik.

In his odyssey Porazik was transferred after a while to another prison in Bohemia where he had to care for prostitutes, then to Slovakia proper, and back and forth. He was surrounded by the dregs of Communist society—a network of brutal sadists, informers and spies. The commander of the infamous labor camp, Nikolaj, greeted them at their arrival with the tirade: "You will all perish here and we will turn your all of your wives into whores and we will reeducate your children so that they will curse you until they die!"

Dr. Neuwirth went through an almost identical ordeal after his arrest on the very same day as Porazik. On the soil of the Medical School and University—once sacred ground and off limits to the authorities—he was arrested by the police and taken to the police station. Also stripped, blindfolded, photographed and fingerprinted, he was transferred to Ruzyňe prison by car and likewise put into solitary confinement. Neuwirth was charged with high treason and espionage for the Vatican and, with the same illegal judicial charade, sentenced on October 15, 1954, to twelve years in prison.

His close friend, Dr. Jenčík, the theologian and priest, was arrested as well while taking a diocesan report from the bishop of Košice to the Archbishop. Jenčík was sentenced to sixteen years imprisonment in the uranium mines of Jáchymov.

At the Medical School the chair of the Department of Chemistry was taken over by Dr. Timotej Turský, a Communist zealot from Bratislava. After his graduation in Bratislava, as one of the privileged Communist avant-garde, he was trained at the Academy of Sciences with academician Dr. Šorm in Prague, and completed his postdoctoral training in Moscow. The chair of Microscopic Anatomy was occupied at first by Porazik's assistant professor, and then finally taken by a Communist from Prague, Dr. Hrubý.

At the time of the seizure of Drs. Porazik and Neuwirth, in the wake of this political cleansing, a handful of assistant professors like Dr. Belák, Dr. Pobiš, and Dr. Eichler were arrested on trumped-up charges. Hand-in-hand with this witch-hunt, the "democratization" of the students at this Medical School cut severely into their numbers, eliminating about 70 of them. A significant anti-Church and anti-religious trend was present in this political crusade representing the class struggle. The main ringleaders in this process were Communists like A. Puža, J. Ondík, W. Fryborský, I. Ivančo, K. Barna, T. Turský, J. Filip, and others such as F. Démant, J. Lukáči, J. Sonderlich, A. Valková, and P. Hoffman.

In 1959 this branch of the Medical School of the University of Bratislava received autonomous status and was named after Pavol J. Šafářík, another Protestant pastor (the first being the Protestant Bishop, J. A. Comenius, the patron of the University of Bratislava) in this Catholic land. Born in Hungary in 1795, Šafářík studied theology and worked in Ujvidek, Hungary, at the high school of the Serbian

Orthodox Church. From there he was dismissed because of his Free-mason membership and lived in misery from some time. Later he was invited to go to Prague as a proponent of "Czechoslovakianism" and Czechified his name to Šafářík, and became part of the Czech national intelligentsia.[23] Interestingly, his credentials as a Protestant minister were not an impediment to receiving this honor at the peak of Com-munist totalitarian regime, thus suggesting ideological sympathies with the personage of Šafářík by the political authorities and indicat-ing a peculiar spiritual or ideological tie between these two elements.

Suddenly, in 1960, both Neuwirth and Porazik were pardoned under the general amnesty of the new Stalinist president of the Czechoslovak Republic, Antonín Novotný. Despite this pardon, neither of them was invited or allowed to return to their previous posi-tions at the Medical School. Porazik, now 47 years old, was deeply scarred and intellectually damaged but not broken. The government assigned him to the Department of Communal Hygiene, a world away from his forte in microscopic anatomy. He rallied his intellectual faculties and acumen and produced over 40 scientific papers in his new field. In these papers, he addressed the environmental problems of the workplace and factories as a consequence of acute air pollution produced by the socialist industrial mega-projects as well as the influence of toxic chemicals—a domain with significant political overtones.

Neuwirth, a fine scientist who survived his ordeal thanks to his deep religious faith, emerged spiritually less scathed. He was assigned to work as a general practitioner in a remote part of hilly northwestern Slovakia. Even there his sharp eye and clinical observance put to use his scientific acumen and he did research relating to a rare genetic affliction. Curiously enough, at a medical conference, by chance Neuwirth met his accuser, Dr. A. Millár, the man whose treachery and ideological zeal put Neuwirth in jail and ruined his professional and personal life. Millár, now nearly ten years older and having survived the purges against Zionists in the mid-1950's, asked Neuwirth for for-giveness and pardon. Nobly, Neuwirth shook the hand that had written the damning letter against him and reassured Millár that he had no ill feelings towards him.

At the time of the Prague Spring in 1968, both Neuwirth and Porazik had high hopes that their cases could be fully disclosed and all the incriminating documents revealed and that they would be fully professionally and personally rehabilitated. The invasion of Czechoslovakia in August of 1968 by the Soviet and Warsaw Pact armies dashed all their expectations.

Neuwirth was eventually allowed to work as an Associate Director at the Chemistry Lab at the third branch of the Medical School. He was originally invited to have a full academic position and appointment, on the provision that he renounce his religious beliefs and relinquish his religious affiliations with the Catholic Church. Neuwirth flatly refused this invitation and took a lesser job at the chemistry laboratory. He then published over 30 papers and did respectable research in his field. He retired in 1986.

Finally the curtain came down on this Communist drama, which U.S. President Ronald Reagan called the "evil empire." In the late fall of 1989, the Communist regime of Czechoslovakia collapsed as the consequence of the "Velvet Revolution" unleashed by students, intellectuals, and dissidents, and playwright Vaclav Havel was named President. In the spring of 1990, both Porazik and Neuwirth were fully rehabilitated by the new democratic government and they were able to see and review their heavy dossiers full of accusations and outright lies and confront the actors. It was finally and unequivocally pronounced that they had been unlawfully arrested and sentenced on trumped-up charges which had been complete forgeries. They were completely rehabilitated both personally and professionally, the emphasis being placed on the fact that they had suffered horrendous consequences and incarceration with terrible repercussions for their families and children as well as tremendous economic hardship.

Dr. Neuwirth was now awarded a gold medal, the highest honor of his Medical School, for his scientific contributions and teaching. Fate was less kind to Dr. Porazik. After rehabilitation he was appointed by President Havel in Prague's famous Carolinum with full honors as a full professor of Microscopic Anatomy. But he was now 67 years old and at the Medical School this towering man was not welcomed by the still-ensconced ruling academia of the former Communist professionals and professors who were chairing their departments undisturbed. There was a complete lack of moral justice and incentive to mitigate, if not rectify, at least partially the terrible ordeal which this decent man had lived through, thanks to his colleagues.

After six months as the Chairman of the Department, the Dean listed his post as open for new applicants with the excuse of his advanced age. It was an unbecoming moral descent on the part of the Dean and a showed a lack of any collegiality for this distinguished scientist. Porazik took his departure from the Medical School in stride but now his health, undermined by years in prison, began to fail. In 1993 he underwent a hip replacement which, either because of inexperience or inappropriate technology, was an obvious surgical failure. Porazik was now on crutches and within a year confined to a wheelchair—a terrible blow to this tall, athletic and still energetic man.

Early in 1995, while under regular medical observation, he started to have bouts of fever, weight loss and other grave symptoms. Significant time was lost while doctors looked for the etiology of his symptoms in his orthopedic problem. Eventually, an advanced and inoperable colon cancer was properly diagnosed. Within a few months this exceptional scientist and human being was dead. At this funeral, his fellow prisoner, Dr. A. Neuwirth, with tears in his eyes chronicled the personal and professional drama of this remarkable man and victim of the times.

These events exemplify how the intellectual elite and cerebral potential and intellectual capacity were wasted. Now, in the 1990's and after the fall of Communism, the victims and the victors in this land can look into each other's eyes, while only the dead martyrs scream, "J'accuse!"

6
Forty Years of "Bolshe Vita"

The Hungarian film director Ibolya Fekete, who won the Hungarian Film Critics prize for her motion picture, *Bolshe Vita* (The Good Life), during an interview with Teresa Agovino, mused about the past (*Newsweek*, September 8, 1997): "In an American movie the hero is the one who is right, and the one who is going to win. In an Eastern European story, the hero is the one who is right, but...he is going to lose." Indeed, in the mid-50's, innocent and decent people were still losing, victims of a political witch-hunt where professionals and scientists with impeccable personal credentials were the ultimate losers.

The virtuous Dr. E. Šteklačová, professor of anatomy, had been dismissed from the Department of Anatomy and the Medical School in Bratislava. Already in her mid-50's and suddenly without a job, she went to work as a salesgirl in a dairy store in an outright display of defiance. The whole city went to see her to boost her morale. Eventually she ended up as a pathologist in a small town in the mountains of Slovakia.

The brilliant neurosurgeon Dr. Jozef Žucha, surrounded by a vicious Communist clique and its ringleader, Dr. Vito Pohl, eventually got the "coup de grâce" from his junior colleague, Dr. Milan Kratochvil and was dismissed from the Medical School. Afterwards he could only work as an attending physician, and not as a teacher. Eventually, after a flashy but short-lived political and professional career, Kratochvil was dropped as well from the Medical School.

The biggest loss in these years was when Professor Dr. František Klein, the maven of pathology, was expelled from his department. His pupil and nemesis, Assistant Professor Miroslav Brosman, breathing down his neck since 1947, took over his Chair in Pathology in 1959 and went on to enjoy an unprecedented and uncontested career, later serving as a top specialist in pathology at the Ministry of Health.

115

Nobody dared to challenge Brosman's aspirations or qualifications. As a consequence of his stressful dismissal from the Medical School, Klein died of a heart attack a year later.

One of my classmates paid dearly for his moral rectitude and courage and eventually lost the fight. In my graduating class of 1952, he was an excellent student but was a city bourgeois. After graduation he, and his apolitical friends from Bratislava, were delegated to work in the most eastern part of Slovakia, close to the border of the Soviet Union. He specialized in obstetrics and quickly advanced in his field. His superior recognized his talents and did not want him to wither in this small hospital and, therefore, recommended him for an appointment as an assistant professor at the Department of Obstetrics at the Medical School in Bratislava in 1956. The following year, according to law No. 68/1957 and by order of the Ministry of Health, law No. 269/1958, abortions were made legal and widely available, paid for by the state health service. My friend, Erwin, was now assigned to perform abortions, an act contrary to his medical and personal conscience. To the consternation of the Medical Staff and the Communist Party clique at the Department, comrades Dušan Brucháč, Mikuláš Toldy and Ján Pavkovič and the professor himself, he refused to perform this procedure. After a stormy tug-of-war on November 4, 1959, Erwin was expelled from the Department and his license was suspended for two years. He made a living by doing manual labor as a stock-boy in a warehouse for six months without pay. Fortunately, his luck started to change in his favor. He switched to anesthesiology and, after many ups and downs, ended up in the United States, eventually becoming an Attending in anesthesiology at a prestigious hospital in New York.

Meanwhile, the victors, the hard-core Communist assistant professors, continued unchallenged and unprecedented careers in the years to come in the fields of their choosing. They were the only ones who traveled for training and meetings to the best institutions in Western Europe and the US, gaining significant professional advancements, and making themselves virtually untouchable and indispensable. They had a master plan for their own future.

The main architects of the new medical and political doctrine, which transformed the Medical School for the next 40 years, grew out of the graduating class of 1950 and eventually fundamentally influenced the health care of the entire country.

One of the most noticeable and prominent of these was Dr. Vladimír Zvara, who chose urology to be his undisputed domain. After training in Prague with the country's best experts, he returned to the Medical School as the heir-apparent and secretary of the chair, becoming the key player in this specialty, where without his approval nothing moved at the Medical School or in the country. His ascendancy to a professorship as part of the Communist *nomenklatura* was unassailable and had the blessing of the Communist Party, of which he was the most influential. It was a self-supporting political loop where they were approved by the Party and yet were the Party as well. It was a masterful and shrewd political stratagem that served them all very well.

Zvara not only dominated the field and Department of Urology but was a most influential member of the Medical School, serving as Associate Dean and then as a plenipotentiary member in the government, as Minister of Health for seven years (1964–1971) without interruption, even after the invasion of the country by Soviet troops in 1968. He survived the test of these political times. One of the most traveled physicians to the "despicable" west, he was eventually honored as Academician, Soviet style, and became a member of the Slovak Academy of Sciences. Of course, he had the privilege to choose and prepare his son for the very same career and specialty, and young Peter Zvara had no difficulty in qualifying for the Medical School.

His comrade-in-arms, the bigmouth Dr. Dušan Bruchác, was a man who marked many lives at the Medical School during these turbulent years. He likewise boosted his career from the outset by training in Prague, which gave him a major push ahead of his contemporaries, who were without these advantages. He also advanced quickly and easily and took over the Department of Obstetrics as part and parcel of the Communist Party. Besides studying in Prague, he visited his idol, the Soviet Union, and France as well. Bruchác was appointed as the highest authority and expert for obstetrics at the Ministry of Health.

Another member of the class of 1950 was Emil Huraj, a lifelong member of the Communist Party, who assaulted his future boss and professor at the famous "active" in May, 1950, for allegedly unethical conduct, thus cornering and putting political pressure on him. Huraj then dominated the field of orthopedics and watched over it like a hawk, ultimately inheriting the chair. An Associate Dean (1961–1963) at the Medical School, as a Communist he boosted his academic prominence entirely by appointment and not by the elective process. He served as Vice-Rector in 1963–1969 and was eventually crowned Rector of the University for a term of seven years (1969–1976). Huraj was also smart enough not only to survive but advance in the political backlash after the Soviet invasion in 1968. Three Soviet medals decorate his chest—from the Universities of Kiev, Leningrad, and Moscow—testifying to his political allegiance. He was also made an honorary Doctor at the University of Halle in East Germany, the staunchest satellite of the Soviet Union.

Two couples sold out the Slovak Academy of Science and its Medical Branch: Zachar-Zacharová (Beliačková) and Gero-Gerova (Jansová), also graduates of the class of 1950. They all spent three years happily training in Prague at the Czechoslovak Academy of Science, choosing basic science as their field of interest. They chose the Academy because it was an institution that was better funded than others were. These scientists also had the unique opportunity to advance their training by studying extensively abroad. While first paying homage to their paragon in science, the Soviet Union, they finally turned to study in the capitalist and decadent West. Zachar achieved his coveted goal of becoming an Academician and a member of the Slovak Academy of Sciences; he also secured his son's future, who not surprisingly followed in his footsteps at the Medical School.

In the early 1980's at a meeting in New York a professional colleague, Dr. Norman Gootman, from the neighboring Long Island Jewish Medical Center approached me. During our informal conversation, he startled me with the question: "Do you know Dr. Gero and his wife, Mária, who are here from your country? They are here to try to set up some mutual research with my wife Phyllis from Downstate Medical Center in Brooklyn." I was taken off guard by this unexpected information and my jaw dropped quickly, turning into a grin that expressed my amusement. Of course I admitted that I knew something about them, without, however, disclosing that they were the crème de la crème of the Communist elite who had the gumption to visit the once-despised ideological enemy. It was over 30 years since they had embarked on their unprecedented careers, which would have been unheard of for the average physician in Slovakia. I was also curious to know what they were working on. Dr. Gootman asked me if I would like to meet them. I did not object and he told me that he would give me a call. But the call never came and I was not surprised. They were probably not thrilled that Gootman had even mentioned their presence in the United States. It seemed to me that times had changed, and with it also the people—or had they?

These examples of the political trickery of this avant-garde were quickly emulated by the subsequent classes at the Medical School, who also wanted to partake of this political and academic harvest and claim their share of professional advancement. After the "victorious" 1948, in my class as in any other, the Communist elite benefited enormously from their affiliations and could pick and choose their field of expertise and achieve spectacular and unchallenged careers without questions or objections being raised regarding the provenance of these tremendous advantages and promotions.

One of the most vicious ringleaders of the Communist sorority was Milota Kohutová-Grešíková, who eliminated many students from our class on the pretense that they admired the achievements and research of Western, and especially US, medicine. A mediocre student, she joined the Communist Party immediately in 1948, trampling on and causing professional and personal harm and anguish to many in that year. What a Communist zealot she turned out to be! After her graduation, Kohutová selected what was the choicest fruit in the country and went to work at the prestigious Institute of Virology at the Slovak Academy of Sciences under the leadership of Professor Dr. Dioniz Blaškovič. Right after graduation, a position was made available for her according the Communist Party plan where she was one of its most important lieutenants.

An unabashed shrew with her ruthless critique and condemnation of the United States as a warmonger and capitalist enemy, she went to study in the US in 1962–63 and received substantial training in research in the field of tick-born diseases, such as Lyme disease, a forte of US virological research. She published her findings about arbor viruses in 1972 in Europe. In 1976 she received the state award of Klement Gottwald, the Communist president. Later on her dream came true when she was awarded the coveted degree of Academician, Soviet style—the only female to ever receive this award.[1]

Another classmate, Gustáv Čatár, also able to choose his field of study, worked in parasitology at the Medical School and at the Academy of Science. Most importantly, he chaired the commission for the structural transformation of the Medical School, following the Soviet model. By appointment and blessing of the Communist Party, and not by election, he served at the Medical School as an Associate Dean (1965–1969), as a Dean for seventeen years (1969–1986), and as the University Vice-Rector during the days of hard-core Communism, thus serving his Party faithfully.

Other members such as Dr. Pavol Mäsiar, who also trained in Prague and became a professor at the Medical School in Košice, spent time in Australia, which was an unreachable dream for any member of the Medical School. Dr. Pavol Duda and Dr. Eva Bullová-Brixová, labeled by some of her classmates as the "blond beast," were the darlings of the Party, who, using their political leverage, were able to achieve enviable careers available only to Communists.

There was an interesting fellow in our class, an excellent student, who used his symbiosis with the Communists and his roots of Russian origin to advance his career. In 1971, coming from Boston where I was a Fellow at the Children's Hospital of Harvard, I attended a World Congress in Cardiology in London. There I was pleased to meet my former professor and teacher and her friend, Professor Dr. Vladimír Haviar. When my classmate noticed me, he shied away and avoided me like the plague throughout the conference. While I had lunch with my countrymen, the two professors, I asked them how it came to be that this junior lecturer, not a Communist Party member, was attending this prestigious meeting in London? They looked at each other meaningfully and then one of them volunteered in a whisper, "You know he can go to any conference that the wants to, because he works as a quisling for the authorities." I let it pass.

In 1984, I met my classmate again in Paris at another World Congress. He was now a professor and chairman of his Department. This time in the lobby we exchanged a courtesy "hello" and "how are you?" I hardly caught his reply when I suddenly noted a "schreck" or look of panic in his eyes. He turned white and blurted out, "Goodbye, I have to go." He made a sharp left turn, and suddenly his face started to beam with an ear-to-ear grin as he approached a bald, burly, middle-aged bear of a man in baggy pants, exclaiming in Russia with open arms: "Welcome, comrade professor," and then shaking his hand wholeheartedly. I stood there stunned and speechless like Lot's wife in the Book of Genesis, who turned into a pillar of salt.

In 1990, after the fall of Communism, I visited Bratislava, going on a bright Sunday morning to a church service at St. Martin's Cathedral. Towards the end of the service, while people were moving about, I glanced to the left and to my surprise and disbelief, I saw my classmate again. My movement evidently made me noticeable because his shadow stealthily faded away into the crowd and vanished toward the exit. I was speechless again and wondered what he was up to now, attending church services.

In the second half of the Communist era, a new generation of Communist youth appeared on the professional scene, the sons and daughters of the "politically correct" leaders and professors at the Medical School. These newly bred juniors, soaked in red ideology, were destined to follow in the footsteps of their forebears and they had no difficulties in being accepted at the University or into higher education, advancing on the conveyer belt already set in motion for them. They were pleased to follow their parents in politicized careers.

On the other hand, their contemporaries, the offspring of the previously democratized and eliminated intelligentsia, mostly Catholic, with the political baggage of their parents which they carried virtually since birth, had absolutely no chance to get into University. They ended up as blue-collar workers and at the lower professional and social end as a consequence of the political remaking of the social order.

This status quo was suddenly interrupted in 1968 with the invasion of the Soviet and Warsaw Pact troops into Czechoslovakia in order to suppress the Communist political meltdown and reform as well as Dubček's "Prague Spring." While some of the Communists at the Medical School supported the political relaxation and reform and stuck out their necks, they paid dearly for their disloyalty—for betraying the Party discipline, they were soon sacked. For example, Dr. Vladimír Maňák, Timotej Turský and Erwin Barta, were dismissed. The diehard Communists, while shaken, took a wait-and-see attitude and eventually were the victors and continued in their political opportunism and academic careers. To the real disappointment of many reform-minded intellectuals, Ladislav Novomeský, now again in the political saddle, kept to the Party's iron discipline and put his signature of consent on approving the Soviet invasion.

From the mid-1970's on, it was evident that the system was in decline and only able to sustain itself by political means. As the "evil empire's" foundations were falling apart at its economic seams, so the Soviet satellites started to crumble as well. In 1987, after about twenty years, I revisited the department where I had once happily worked with great drive and enthusiasm. Almost in secrecy, I entered the country wanting to see where the benchmark of medical science stood. I visited the three Medical Schools where some of my residents were now in advanced positions and allowed me to look behind the official veil. I was received by some of my former colleagues with unease. We walked through the hospital, which had not changed or improved in its physical make-up until we came to the laboratory, which had once been my pride and which I had been in charge of. It was a surprising encounter, a mixture of being moved to see all the machinery which I had worked with still there, being able to touch the dials and consoles which made me reconnect with my youth, and at the same time it was an appalling sight to see the dilapidated state of all these totally obsolete machines which were virtually useless. It was dismaying, yet at the same time, it seemed a miracle that this younger generation of doctors could work in these run-down conditions. And what about their patients? What unknown risks and dangers were they faced with and exposed to with this ancient technology? And this was the only center in the land for the diagnosis of heart problems for children. The equipment and technology was three decades behind the requirements of the times. Health care was obviously not the priority of the Communist system and was visibly and terribly underfunded. What had once been the pride of Slovakia from the early 1950's on, when cardiac surgery for children and adults was founded by Professor Dr. Karol Šiška and his cardiologist associates, Professor Dr. Vladimír Haviar and my teacher, Professor Dr. Irena Jakubcová, what I now saw showed a significant decline and regression of this important clinical specialty. I had to question very gingerly what their ultimate results were, not wanting to offend the feelings of these colleagues who had to work under such dire conditions. The leaders of medicine, tied by their political affiliations, did not dare reveal that their patients with heart conditions had a very poor chance of survival compared to patients in Western Europe, let alone in the United States. The general public, isolated by the Iron Curtain, knew nothing about these matters.

A dramatic episode comes to mind when, in the early 1960's, I was taking care of a beautiful 10-year-old boy. He was the son of a State Secretary of Development in the central government in Prague. The boy had a severe heart condition for which treatment was available only in the US. The Surgeon General, in order to get the agreement of the Communist government to allow the boy's treatment in the US, would have to sign a document that the treatment was not available in Czechoslovakia. He was, of course, a political appointee and even though the boy's father was a Communist bigwig, the surgeon did not have the courage to make a statement to the top leaders which would disclose the inferior state of the health care system which was regarded by the Communist Party as the best in the world. The boy limped through life until an infection of the abnormal valve killed him at the age of twenty. Of course, the average citizen had it much worse, while the Communists had their own "state sanatorium" where they enjoyed the best conditions and treatment that the country could offer—but only for the Communist elite. Under Communism, all citizens were equal, except for the elite.

Then, in November 1989, almost unforeseen and to the disbelief of the Communist *nomenklatura* and its leaders, the Communist system in Czechoslovakia and in the neighboring countries collapsed. Nobody knew how to react to this rapturous new development and what to expect. At least at the Medical School and the University, almost every professional remained in place with only some minor cosmetic changes, continuing with the old routine and a wait-and-see attitude.

The end result of the previous forty years was that most of the political professors were now difficult to replace because there was no alternative intelligentsia waiting in the wings, and thus the old guard was the best that was available. The issues were enormous and complex. These people had survived this 40-year period and so virtually everybody was tainted by the smoldering "slow virus" of Communism, even at the lowest level. In the leading strata of professionals, nobody wanted to talk about the shameful past or face it. How much should be made known and public? Should the victors of the past be allowed to keep their posts? What about the victims of the past and their offspring? The winners in the past were for no changes at all. They did not need new people—their goal was to turn the page, no questions asked, with no catharsis of the system. It was the system that was blamed and not the people who made it or profited from it, and there was no repentance, but rather arrogance, from the former champions. The so-called law of "lustration," calling former ringleaders to claim responsibility for their past actions, or prevent them from maintaining the advantages of their high posts, was adroitly thwarted and suspended in Slovakia and pushed under the rug.[2] It never led to a showdown or confrontation of the leaders of the totalitarian system, not even in order to look them straight in the eye.

There was really no fundamental change of the guard as had occurred in 1945, when Fascism was defeated. This was not a French revolution, where heads would roll—this was a "velvet" revolution. A new generation will have to come forward in the future with the courage to delve into the turbulent past and from it draw lessons and conclusions. The current leading strata is unwilling and unable to do the job.

Presently, a transitional generation is coming onto the professional scene and many of these, if not the majority, are the offspring of the founding fathers of the Communist dictatorship who initiated the tremendous social overhaul in 1948. On the medical scene and at the Medical School, names like Zvara, Nikš, Brix, Krsek, Šiška and Zachar appear as these extensions of their parents stake their own claims on the professional turf. They inherited information about how to get ahead and how to get a stipend for work in the West, information that they kept mostly to themselves. It was barely after the fall of Communism, in 1991, when one of these heirs, Dr. Peter Zvara, applied for a stipend from an American-Czechoslovak institution, which was truly audacious coming from a man with his Communist legacy. These young turncoats showed no inhibitions, and stole virtually all of the coveted places offered in the West because they were the only ones privy to this information. They are working in Western Europe, England and the US as well, and acquiring endless professional advantages thereby. One can only hope that they will also learn something about democracy and professional integrity, which they will apply in the future.

The offspring of the "democratized" victims of the early 1950's had no chance! They received the best that could be expected, such as a formal apology from the Rector of the University for all the injustices and suffering which they—close to 1,000 dismissed students—had to endure with their families. It was too little and too late, and making a full reversal of the dirty past was really impossible. There was no solution and no remedy.[3]

In 1990 I became interested in at least getting an approximate overview or picture of the present status of some of the medical practices or science and its impact on the health care of the average citizen. In developed societies, such as Czechoslovakia, the society by and large faces similar health problems in at least two major fields. The leading concern remains the affliction of cardiovascular morbidity and mortality while the second major medical liability in the modern world is the detection and curtailment of medical malignancies. Life expectancy is obviously affected by these two major medical problems, which significantly influence the quality of life and are sources of the biggest health care expenditures of society. In ischemic heart disease, the introduction of coronary bypass surgery in 1967 in the United States was a major turning point in the treatment of coronary heart disease. Since then, hundreds of thousands of patients have been saved and their quality of life changed.

In 1990 I inquired about this particular procedure as an indicator or litmus test of the status of medical practice in this common and major heart problem. I learned then that coronary bypass surgery was not available there, indicating a quarter of a century lag between Slovakia and the US or other Western countries. Also at that time, no interventional cardiology was available and the surgical treatment of children born with heart problems was not much better.

I further searched to see if there were any measures being taken or publicized in preventing cardiovascular morbidity and if the medical practitioners inquired into risk factors such as a positive family history for myocardial infarction or stroke, cigarette smoking, high cholesterol and blood pressure or diabetes. Curiously, one of the leading pathologists and his wife had been interested in these measures and were even supplied with relevant literature. But by and large I learned that there was no concentrated effort in the prevention of this major health problem at the basic level of medical professionals, let alone the public, where even the university-educated segment remains woefully uninformed.

It was difficult for me to get hard information about the status of the art or therapeutic results in the field of malignancies. This is sometimes difficult to assess, even in the United States where only now the first definitive signs of cures and the trend to potential victory in these fields are beginning to be seen. Therefore, I tried to learn about the availability of the preventive measures at the physician- and patient-level of the mostly university-educated public.

In females the greatest menace is breast cancer and preventative measures such as regular mammograms, which have been practiced in the West for decades, are woefully underutilized or at best spotty in Slovakia. Pap smears for cancers of the reproductive organs in post-menopausal women are virtually unknown. In Urology, clinical examinations, not to mention blood tests to detect the scourge of prostate cancer in men, are likewise unknown. Early detection for colon cancer or preventative measures for lung cancer, which address the rampant smoking problem in men and women, do not even scratch the surface of what should be faced. It seems that the Ministry of Health, in the past, did not keep pace with the civilized world.

These simple indicators demonstrate significant deficiencies and a lag in the practice of Communist medicine of the past. There appears to be a lack of patient-oriented research and a disassociation of laboratory research by the Academy of Science from the clinical research in medical institutions. There seems to be a wide gap between the plethora of theoretical publications of many candidates and doctors of science, and their impact on the fundamentals of health care for the average citizen in these two major areas of public health.

Some distinguished medical authorities indicate as well that the isolation of the country from Western science and the lack of professional ethics and Hippocratic philosophy led to extensive plagiarism, which seemed to be widespread behind the Iron Curtain where copyright laws were neither sacred nor respected. I am aware that Dr. A. Chura's *Textbook of Respiratory Diseases in Children* and Dr. F. Švec's *Pharmacology* text were translated by the Soviets without any respect to their copyright. But they ran into an international scandal with litigation when they published Dr. G. Franconi's *Textbook of Pediatrics* from Switzerland without the copyright. They had to face a large judgment and international condemnation as well. It seems to be that not infrequently in the Eastern Bloc, this was the usual way of doing business—not accepting, let alone respecting, the rules of the West. Not surprisingly, the Slovak medical society was not immune to the temptation to take someone else's intellectual property and present it as their own.

In 1982, the leading authority of the land, Dr. Daniel Bartko, a professor of neurology, published a textbook of neurology. It was a verbatim translation of a text published in West Germany in 1973. It was eight years before this fraud was exposed and the professor brought to justice and responsibility—that is, after the fall of Communism. According to the document of the Prosecutor of Bratislava dated October 3, 1990, in order to enrich himself, this professor was also involved in other shenanigans and shady financial transactions. While he had to leave the Medical School, he escaped prosecution because the president of Czechoslovakia, Václav Havel, declared an amnesty for all past transgressions and the case was closed.

I was personally aware of another case of intellectual piracy whereby a lecturer copied twenty pages of a text and computer-produced figures not available in Slovakia from a US textbook on disturbances of the heart-rhythm in children. When the Dean of the school was made aware of this transgression, the case was hushed up. And these are probably only some of the most blatant examples of plagiarism.

Another interesting trend of questionable professional ethics is the nonchalant translation of the Soviet-style degree, Candidate of Science (C.Sc.), into the venerated research degree of Ph.D. in the United States. While the former is a degree of a postdoctoral thesis with significant ideological underpinnings and, at best, an overview of a medical topic with little scientific value, the latter is mostly a degree in laboratory science in Medicine, which is scarcely ever aspired to by clinicians. Yet it is the highest award and the pinnacle of science earned only after many years of hard work and strenuously contested by the best authorities in the field, who are totally disassociated from the researcher professionally and personally. Cronyism to achieve this degree is unthinkable and would be regarded as the gravest ethical

breach with severe professional consequences. On the other hand, professional cronyism in Eastern Bloc countries is known to be rampant.

These unbecoming descents in professional ethics that punctuate
the medical-academic scene in Eastern Bloc countries mirror a severe
undercurrent of ethical deformation. Now, the restoration of professional honor should be the highest priority according to classical
academic and democratic rules under which fair play should be
reconstituted in the medical field and in society.

While visiting the country of my origin, I got involved in trying
to help and boost the professional potentials and expertise of about
half a dozen of the members of the new generation of doctors by
trying to prod them into going to the United States for training in
medical fields. While some of the older colleagues were funded and
sent for advanced training to Canada, England, and the US, the
younger group was encouraged to attempt to jump the high hurdle of a
exam which would allow them to apply for training positions in the
US. In 1967, at the American embassy in Prague, I also faced this
formidable hurdle, the ECFMG exam (Educational Council for
Foreign Medical Graduates), where a dozen of us from all parts of
Czechoslovakia sweated the exam in order to submit an application
for training positions in the US.

I had high hopes that this young elite, who were at the top of their
class, would do as well as we had done in 1967, when the passing rate
was about 80%. All textbooks were provided and expenses for the
tests were covered for this young group from Bratislava. Even though
these junior colleagues did not try to take the exam in one package,
splitting it into the basic sciences and clinical part, which was per-
fectly legitimate, the passing rate was still disappointing and even
repeated attempts ended in failure. As I learned later, this was the case
in other Eastern European countries and was not unique for Slovakia.
I was sincerely sorry and understood the hardship and heartbreak of
this group of very nice people, but unfortunately it was evidence that
the Medical School did not prepare these candidates for the rigor of
these exams in the West, as had been the case a quarter of a century
ago.

These were all worrisome signs and indications of the level of
medical science and its teaching during the Communist decades. By
chance I reviewed a paper by Dr. Mikuláš Mikulecký from Bratislava,

who quoted David Pendlebury (*Scientist*, October 1988) who unveiled the science of "the eastern block." According to Mikulecký's reference and analysis of the years 1973–1987, it was possible to conclude that our (Czechoslovak) science had the worst relentlessly declining trend.

In another vein, while reviewing the past achievements of the University of J. A. Comenius in Bratislava during the first 75 years of its existence through the eyes of Slovak historians, my attention turned to the chapter on the Honorary Doctors of the University.[4] This honorary degree, representing the highest accolade of the University, was bestowed on 77 illustrious men with supposedly impeccable professional achievements and personal characteristics. Interestingly, not one woman achieved this honor, which perhaps reflects the history of the times in this convoluted part of Europe. I am convinced that some outstanding contenders will soon be considered.

It was moving for me that the founding fathers of the University revealed their great wisdom and moral rectitude by bestowing the first honorary degree of the University in 1928 on R. Seton-Watson, who put Slovakia's plight and grievances on the international scene when he acquainted the world with the massacre at Černová in 1905.

Up until 1939, seventeen honorary doctorates were awarded, including one in 1937 to Dr. E. Beneš, the Czech politician and the president of Czechoslovakia. While he was a skilled politician, his personal character was another matter. The following year another politician, Dr. Milan Hodza, the Prime Minister of the Republic, received this award. These recipients seem to indicate that political undercurrents had more than a negligible influence on the selection of the men that the University decided to honor.

During the interwar Slovak Republic, only two honorary degrees were awarded. After 1945 I noticed the names of Professor Dr. St. Kostlivý and Professor Dr. K. Hynek, the founders and pioneers of the Medical School.

During the forty years following the "victorious February" of 1948, thirty-seven honorary degrees were bestowed, and interestingly enough one-third of these were given to men from the Soviet Union. Without questioning the professional merit or personal attributes of this group, the obvious disproportion in the distribution of these awards makes me question the purity of the decisions made by the senior members of the University and hint at considerable ideological compromise.

In 1969 Ladislav Novomeský, the controversial bard-politician, received this honor even though he scarred or destroyed the careers and lives of many decent human beings in a thoroughly dishonorable manner. That this honor was bestowed upon him after the invasion of the Soviet and Warsaw Pact armies, which he approved, is probably no accident.

After the "Velvet Revolution" in 1989, the first honorary doctorate was awarded to Václav Havel, a man of integrity and impeccable personal character who is internationally known as a distinguished playwright. Havel was a dissident and became the President of the new Czechoslovakia. This seemed to convey the important message that the sages of the University had begun a new chapter for the future. Alexander Dubček, the tragic Communist with a human face and Slovak with the soul of a dove, was honored the following year.

It gave me a thrill to see two illustrious Americans honored. They were Jaroslav J. Pelikán, of Slovak descent, from Yale University, and Eugene A. Cernan, who as the last astronaut to walk on the moon. His father was Slovak and his mother Czech.

But then a time-bomb exploded before my eyes when I noticed the name of Professor Dr. Karol Rebro, in 1993. He was the lawyer who had marked the lives of so many professors after 1945 at the Medical School, and destroyed so many promising careers of Christian students after 1948. One has to wonder about the thought process which put this professor, with his checkered past, on the highest pedestal of honor of the University, in line with many others who indeed had an irreproachable character and personal record. What a telltale sign and reflection of the times in this fatally flawed decision-making process, where the men who knew Rebro's background forgot their responsibility to reward only the best. This indeed seemed like an ironic reversal of Ibolya Fekete's reasoning in her movie, *Bolshe Vita*, where the bad guy was nevertheless honored as a winner.

Epilogue

The historic drama played out in the second half of the twentieth century in Czechoslovakia was the most poignant and intense in the annals of the country.

The pageant of Comenius University, starting from its humble beginnings in 1919, acutely mirrored the historical scene through its Czecho-Slovak years, the Slovak Republic and the reestablishment of Czechoslovakia as well, and in 1948 its takeover by the Communists and its 40 years under a totalitarian regime with all its consequences. These last 40 years under Communism had the most far-reaching political, economic and, most importantly, social consequences in the life of the Medical School and the University as well as the entire society.

In the first chapter of the existence of the University, there were major conceptual tensions and struggles over the idea of what "national" meant for these people. A clash arose between the official "Czechoslovak" ideology and the national Slovak distinctiveness and its desirable political, economic, and social consequences. The ideological-political fault line between the Protestant minority and the Catholic majority (some 70% of the population of Slovakia) was, tragically, not the only dispute which split this nation, fostered by the mirage and political deceit of a Czechoslovak nation. Later it planted the seeds for the cozy affiliation of the more liberal Protestants with the onslaught of the Communist Party via Prague after 1945. This was, of course, a defining moment, as was 1948, which sealed the fate for the mostly Catholic Slovaks behind the Iron Curtain for a half century with unforeseen consequences and a historic outcome.

During the wartime Slovak Republic, the nationhood of the majority attained the coveted embodiment of the "national" but its expression was compromised under the preposterous political circumstances and the Second World War. Yet the University retained a significant latitude and breathing space to maintain its functional integrity.

After 1945 there was a worldwide regrouping and polarization of political allegiances and powers and Czechoslovakia fell into the Soviet sphere of interest. The Czechoslovak Republic was reestablished and immediately a period of political repercussions of an unprecedented ferocity followed. Political allegiances of the past were treated as criminal offenses, especially on the stage of the University. Absent due legal process, many professional lives were ruined in this first round of political cleansing—an event where many personal accounts were settled.

These political assassinations were harbingers of worse things to come after the "victorious" February of 1948 when the Communists took over Czechoslovakia with the help of the Soviet Union. Several waves of political cleansing followed on the national scene as well as at the Medical School and University. Innocent professors' and students' lives were ruined and 350,000 Slovaks and Czechs were jailed or sent to labor camps.[1]

According to Tina Rosenberg, in 1950 some 244 people were executed, 8,500 died in penal institutions—most of them tortured—and 140,000 were jailed for deeds perpetrated against the Communist state.[2] This all occurred in the name of establishing a new social order in the country based on Marxist-Leninist ideology and class struggle.

As time proved, Marxism-Leninism was a major mistake in the history of mankind.[3] It claimed to be a scientific ideology, but proved to be an unsubstantiated, empty slogan that suppressed any contradictory thinking and maintained a false front.[4] Marxism-Leninism was supposed to be the covenant for a new social order, free from exploitation and inequality, advancing mankind to a higher plane in the annals of history.[5] Instead it divided society into "them, "the feared and contemptible nomenclature, and "us," the citizens at their mercy.[6]

At the University it created an unprecedented social dislocation of its professionals by political means for political ends. A direct result was the deformation and lowering of professional standards and the destruction of professional integrity. The farce played out at the University setting was even more dramatic since the actors were educated men and women who should have borne a higher accountability for their deeds.

The educational system was used to transform the citizen and the social structure to the idealized Soviet model, which was a total fraud.[7] The professional nomenclature enjoyed unparalleled privileges and transmitted these advantages to their offspring and relatives without compunction. This secretive elite demonstrated an enormous discrepancy between their proclaimed political virtues and their real conduct.[8] These "untouchables" had secret connections to the Central Committee of the Communist Party, or were actually members of it, and also had secret dealings with the police.[9] Every organ of government, institutions of education, and mass organizations were subordinated to the Communist Party and its Marxist-Leninist ideology with its anti-religious underpinnings. The whole legacy bred tremendous demoralization, duplicitousness and cronyism.

Yet after twenty years of this regime, the professional and moral decay of its citizens demonstrated that the society couldn't function on slogans but needed actual work and output. The "Prague Spring" triggered the invasion of the Soviet and Warsaw Pact armies and was followed by a new wave of purges of the now reform-minded Communists. Some 150,000 citizens who had been in favor of reform of the Communist system were eliminated or marginalized from public and political life.[10] The University and Medical School did not escape unscathed from this wave of purges where the daring perished while the hard-core opportunists remained in the driver's seat. A call for "normalization" was issued, which was nothing more than a preposterous label for the return to the totalitarian era of the not-so-distant past.

Another twenty years were needed until the Communist system and the Soviet "evil empire" collapsed for good. The Communist Party, which had extolled the dream of social justice, revealed itself to have completely betrayed a beautiful idea. Its members, the nomenclature, emerged as the cynical traitors of this utopian ideal. They displayed an glaring contrast between the official canon of Communist values and their professional and personal actions.

Daily existence in the Communist period had tremendous moral ramifications: no one escaped the impact of living with falsehood. Everyone had to make compromises with the regime in order to survive. There were no heroes, only victims.[11] As Rosenberg chronicles, "The quintessential citizen was born during the past era, holding his tongue, carrying out little pieces which the system allowed."[12] The grim circumstances led to many betrayals between friends and colleagues in order to advance one's own career. Most importantly, the citizenry lost its attachment to the precious value of personal honesty, a value once cherished and esteemed. The landscape was full of political dead bodies, a decrepit economy in crisis, social and moral disorientation and decay. For the citizens of Slovakia, it was impossible simply to disassociate from the past, which loomed large, as its heritage was too fresh and overwhelming.

It is impossible to foresee what social forces, institutions or religions will try to rehabilitate the social structure because the latent virus of Communism will linger for a long time in the bone marrow of the population at large. Slovak society achieved democracy through the contributions of a few and the default of many. The population has not yet had the time and courage to examine the past, let alone reject it.[13] The tremendous task of building a political, economic and social order in the framework of democracy lies ahead.

As Karl Popper said, "One chooses democracy not because it abounds with virtues but in order to avoid tyranny."[14] According to Ted Gurr, in the Western definition of democracy there are three essentially independent elements: (1) the presence of institutions and procedures through which the citizen can express preferences about alternative political policies and leaders; (2) the existence of institutional constraints on the exercise of power by the executive branch of government; and (3) the guarantee of civil liberties to all citizens in their daily lives and in acts of political participation.[15] These principles will lead to a "civic" society where the citizen is confident of his rights, tolerant of the plurality of opinions, and a participant rather than a subject of the state.[16] It will take time until this population, the "demos," will rise to the task and correct its moral compass to reach the elusive goal of a decent society.

Notes

Preface

1. Historians in Slovakia have slowly stared to expose the actions of the Communists in various spheres of life. See, for instance, Ján Pešek, *Šťatna bezpečnosťna Slovensku, 1948-1954* (Bratislava: VEDA, 1996), which details the activities of the secret police; František Vnuk, *Vládi zmocnenci na biskupských úradoch v rokoch 1949–1951* (Martin: Matica Slovenská, 1999), which tells how communists infiltrated the Dioceses of Slovakia; and Ján Pešek and Michal Barnovský, *Pod Kuratelou moci: Cirkvi na Slovensku v rokoch 1953–1970* (Bratislava: VEDA, 1999), which tells how the Communists persecuted religion in Slovakia.

Introduction

1. Personal recollection of the author.

Chapter 1: Proscenium in History – The Slovaks

1. For a quick overview of Slovak history, see Stanislav J. Kirshbaum, *A History of Slovakia: The Struggle for Survival* (New York: St. Martin's Press, 1995). For more on Samo's Empire, see Fraňo Tiso, "The Empire of Samo (623–658)," *Slovak Studies* I (1961): 1-21; and for the Great Moravian Empire, see Matús Kučera, *Postavy veľkomoravskej histórie* (Martin: Osveta, 1985).

2. For more on the works of Sts. Cyril and Methodius, see Michal Lacko, *Sts. Cyril and Methodius* (Rome: Slovak Institute, 1969) and Richard Marsina, *Metodov boj* (Bratislava: Obzor, 1985). For the impact of these missionaries on the Slovaks, see Imrich Kruzliak and Francis Mizenko, eds., *SS. Cyril and Methodius Among the Slovaks* (Middleton, PA: Slovak Catholic Federation, 1985).

3. For a comprehensive history of the Slovaks during this period, see Samuel Cambel et al., *Dejiny Slovenska I (do roku 1526)* (Bratislava: VEDA, 1986), and by the same group of authors, *Dejiny Slovenska II (1526–1848)* (Bratislava: VEDA, 1987). For a history of Hungary, see Peter Sugar, ed., *A History of Hungary* (Bloomington: Indiana University Press, 1990).

4. For the history of the Reformation in Slovakia, see David P. Daniel, "Highlights of the Lutheran Reformation in Slovakia," *Concordia Theological Quarterly* 42:1 (January, 1978): 21-34; for a history of the Jesuits in Slovakia, see Emil Krapka and Vojtech Mikula, eds., *Dejiny Spoločnosti Ježisovej na Slovensku, 1561–1988* (Cambridge, Ontario: Dobrá kniha, 1990); for the Jesuit University in Trnava, see Viliam Čičaj, comp., *Trnavská universita v slovenskych dejinách* (Bratislava: SAV, 1987); and for a general history of the Christian Church in Slovakia, see J. Ch. Korec, *Cirkev v dejinách Slovenska* (Bratislava: LUČ, 1989).

5. For more on Bernolák, see Juraj Chovan, ed., *Pamätnica Antona Bernoláka* (Martin: Matica Slovenská, 1992).

6. For an intelligent discussion of this problem, see Peter Brock, *The Slovak National Awakening: An Essay in the Intellectual History of East Central Europe* (Toronto: University of Toronto Press, 1976).

7. For more on Ľudovit Štur, see Jozef Paučo, "Slovakia's Mid-Nineteenth Century Struggle for National Life," *Slovak Studies* 1 (1961): 69-83 and Peter Petro, *A History of Slovak Literature* (Montreal: McGill University Press, 1995): 65-70.

8. The best description of Magyarization can be found in Scotus Viator [R. W. Seton-Watson], *Racial Problems in Hungary* (London: Archibald & Constable, 1908; reprinted in New York by Howard Fertig in 1972). For a detailed history of this period, see Samuel Cambel et al., *Dejiny Slovenska III (od roku 1848 do konca 19. storočia* (Bratislava: VEDA, 1992).

9. For differing perspectives on the Pittsburgh Agreement, see Victor S. Mamatey, "The Slovaks and the Carpatho-Ruthenians," in *The Immigrant's Influence on Wilson's Peace Policies*, ed. by Joseph P. O'Grady (Lewisburg, KY: University of Kentucky Press, 1967): 224-249; and M. Mark Stolarik, "The Role of American Slovaks in the Creation of Czecho-Slovakia, 1914–1918," *Slovak Studies* VIII (1968): 7-82.

10. For Masaryk's repudiation of the Pittsburgh Agreement, see his *The Making of a State* (London: George Allen & Unwin, 1927; reprinted in New York by Howard Fertig, 1969), p. 208. The Slovak struggle for autonomy was best told by James R. Felak in *At the Price of the Republic: Hlinka's Slovak People's Party, 1929–1938* (Pittsburgh: University of Pittsburgh Press, 1994).

11. The best descriptions of this period are Pavol Čarnogurský, *6. október 1938* (Bratislava: VEDA, 1993) and by the same author, *14. marec 1939* (Bratislava; VEDA, 1995). For a longer view, see Carol Skalnik Leff, *National Conflict in Czechoslovakia: The Making and Remaking of a State, 1918–1987* (Princeton: Princeton University Press, 1988).

13. For the breakup of the Republic, see Carol Skalnik Leff, *The Czech and Slovak Republics: Nation Versus State* (Boulder, CO: Westview Press, 1997).

Chapter 2: The University – Between the Two Wars

1. J. Benke, *Medical University of Pécs: A Historical Review* (Pécs: University Press Pécs, 1991), p. 7.

2. Milan Beniak and Miloslav Tichý, *Dejiny Lekárskej Fakulty Univerzity Komenského v Bratislave* (Bratislava: Univerzita Komenského, 1992), p. 24.

3. *Ibid.*, p. 23.

4. *Ibid.*, p. 26.

5. Owen V. Johnson, *Slovakia 1918–1938: Education and the Making of the Nation* (New York: Columbia University Press, 1985), p. 219.

6. Beniak and Tichý, p. 27.

7. J. Horejší, "Vedecká osobnost profesora Kristiana Hynka, 1879–1960" *Čas. Lek. Šek.* 118 (1979): 1149-1152.

8. Beniak and Tichý, p. 27.

9. Benke, p. 7.

10. Beniak and Tichý, p. 28.

11. Johnson, p. 239.

12. *Ibid.*, p. 229.

13. *Ibid.*, p. 223.

14. Beniak and Tichý, pp. 50, 51.

15. *Ibid.*, pp. 66, 67, 69.

16. *Ibid.*, p. 70.

17. Johnson, p. 240.

18. *Ibid.*, pp. 240, 409.
19. I. Kutlík, "K. polstoročnému výrociu smrti Júliusa A. Ladzianského," *Bratislavské Lekárske Listy* 94 (1993): 133-135.
20. Johnson, p. 410.
21. *Ibid.*, p. 241.
22. Beniak and Tichý, p. 87.
23. Horejší, p. 1149.
24. Beniak and Tichý, p. 80.
25. M. Ondrejička, "K nedožitým devatdesiatinám akademika Ladislav Dérera," *Vnitřní Lekařství* 11 (1987): 1031-1035.
26. Beniak and Tichý, p. 83.
27. Loren R. Graham, *Science in Russia and the Soviet Union* (Cambridge University Press, 1933), p. 239.
28. The Pittsburgh Agreement, on May 30, 1918, in which the Czech and Slovak immigrants agreed to create a new Czecho-Slovak Republic.
29. J. Pleva and M. Tichý, "Vývin Lekárskej Fakulty Univerzity Komenského v rokoch 1919-1969," in B. Varsík, ed., *50 rokov Univerzity Komenského* (Bratislava: Univerzita Komenského, 1969), p. 38.
30. M. Tichý and I. Riečanský, "Osobnosť Akademika Dérera," *Čs. zdravotnictví* 35 (1937): 526-532.
31. I. Sečanský, *Spomienky a Vyznanie Lekára* (Bratislava: Slovak Academic Press, 1997), pp. 114, 217, 225.
32. *Ibid.*, p. 158.
33. I. Sečanský, "Akademik Ladislav Dérer," *Zdravie* 44 (1987): 4-7.
34. Ondrejička, p. 1033.
35. R. Korec, "Prof. MUDr. Jozef Skotnický 80 ročný," *Bratislavské Lekárske Listy* 91 (1990): 739.
36. J. Čársky, D. Hermanová, and M. Tichý, "Sto rokov od narodenia Prof. Ing. Dr. tech. Františka Valentiná," *Bratislavské Lekárske Listy* 93 (1992): 219-221.
37. E. Sedláčková and L. Pavlíková, "Prof. MUDr. František Šubík na Lekárskej Fakulty v rokoch 1924-1945," *Slovenský Lekár* 17 (1993): 63-64.
38. F. Inczinger, "K sedemdesiatinám Profesora Františka Šveca," *Čs. Farmacie* 15 (1966): 452.
39. M. Tichý, V. Hrková, M. Kriška, and D. Hermanová, "Pôsobenie Prof. MUDr. Františka Šveca na Lekárskej Fakulty Univerzity Komenského v rokoch 1925-1948," *Bratislavské Lekárske Listy* 93 (1992): 149-152.
40. E. Sedlačková, "75 rokov Lekárskej Faculty Univerzity Komenského v Bratislave," *Recipe* 3 (1994): 37.
41. M. Tichý, L. Pavlíková, A. Kapellerová, and A. Schmídová, "Pôsobenie profesora MUDr. Alojza Churu na Lekárskej Fakulty Univerzity Komenského v Bratislave," *Bratislavské Lekárske Listy* 93 (1992): 203-207.
42. F. R. Perino, "Egas Monis, Founder of Psychosurgery, Creator of Angiography," *Journal International of Coll. Surgery* 36 (1961): 261-272.
43. Beniak and Tichý, p. 107.
44. Konštantín Čársky, *Chirurg Spomína* (Slovenské Spisovatel, 1987), p. 206.
45. D. Duráník and E. Sedláčková, "Sto rokov od narodenia prvého slovenského profesora zubného lekarstva," *Nemocnica* 1 (1996): 26-27.

46. J. Porubský, "Profesor MUDr. Herman Krsek 70 ročný," *Lekársky Obzor* 16 (1967): 591-592.
47. Johnson, p. 331.
48. *Ibid.*, p. 265.
49. Personal communication.
50. Johnson, p. 205.

Chapter 3: Under the Red Flag – or Homo Homini Lupus

1. Ladislav Novomeský, *Desatročia do chvíľ skľbené: Jar v Pešti* (Bratislava: Smena, 1984), p. 18.
2. Karol Rosenbaum, *Ladislav Novomeský, 1904-1974* (Martin: Matica Slovenská, 1974), p. 236.
3. Personal communication.
4. Personal communication.
5. I. Kutlík, "História Vývoja Patologickej Anatomie na Slovensku," *Bratislavské Lekárske Listy* 42 (1962): 415-436.
6. *Encyklopédia Slovenska* (Bratislava: VEDA, 1986), p. 663.
7. *Zápisnice zo zasadania profesorského zboru*, 22.12.1950.
8. *Ibid.*, 2.2.1951.
9. *Ibid.*, 24.1.1952.
10. Personal communication.
11. Júlia Hautová, *Comenius University, 1919–1994* (Bratislava), p. 62.
12. *Ibid.*, p. 62.

Chapter 4: Democratization of the Students or Social Engineering Soviet Style

1. Personal communication.
2. "Zápisnice zo zasadania profesorského zboru." Speech at the IX. Communist Party Congress, 5.25.1949.
3. W. G. Rothstein, *American Medical Schools and the Practice of Medicine: A History* (New York: Oxford University Press, 1987), p. 143.

Chapter 5: The Eastern Massacre

1. O. R. Halaga, "20 rokov Lekárskej Fakulty Univerzity P. J. Šafárika v Košiciach. 1948–1968," *Slovenské Pedagogické Nakladateľstvo* (Bratislava), pp. 31, 32.
2. *Ibid.*, p. 35.
3. *Ibid.*
4. *Ibid.*, p. 39.
5. *Ibid.*, p. 41.
6. A. Kohút and J. Lacko, "40 rokov Lekárskej Fakulty P. J. Šafárika," *Folia Fac. med. Safarikianae Cassoviensis* (1998) 1: 11-21.
7. I. Jurkovič and R. Pospíšil, "K 45 výročiu založenia Lekárskej Fakulty Univerzity P. K. Šafárika," *Folia Fac. med. Safarikianae Cassoviensis* (1993) 1:9-15.
8. *Encyklopédia Slovenska* (Bratislava: VEDA, 1981), p. 437.
9. M. Mydlík, "Tradícia memoriálov Prof. MUDr. Frantiska Póra," *Vnitřní Lekařství* 22 (1998): 176-177.
10. *Encyklopédia Slovenska* (1981), p. 493.
11. Jurkovič and Pospíšil, p. 10.

12. Kohút and Lacko, p. 12.
13. Jurkovič and Pospíšil, p. 13.
14. R. Vrba and Alan Bestic, *I Cannot Forget* (Sidwick and Jackson and Antony Gibbs and Phillips, 1963), p. 212.
15. Graham, pp. 124-126.
16. Personal communication.
17. J. Rapaport, "Krátky život «živé hmoty»," *Nauka z žizň* 9 (1988): 165-168.
18. *Ibid.*, p. 166.
19. *Ibid.*, p. 167.
20. Personal communication.
21. Personal communication.
22. Personal communication.
23. R. W. Seton-Watson, *Documents II. Ústav T. G. Masaryka* (Matica Slovenská, 1996), p. 116.

Chapter 6: Forty Years of "Bolshe Vita"

1. *Encyklopédia Slovenska* (1981), p. 196.
2. Tlačova Agentúra Slovenskej Republiky, "Lustračný zákon na Slovensku už neplatí," *Sme/Smena* (1997) 3: 1.
3. Juraj Švec, "Vysokoskolské Requiem," *Svedectvo* (1992) 3: 4.
4. Hautová, p. 105.

Epilogue

1. Tina Rosenberg, *The Haunted Land* (New York: Random House, 1995), p. 10.
2. *Ibid.*, p. 70.
3. Ernest Gellner, *Conditions of Liberty* (New York: The Penguin Press, 1994), p. 30.
4. *Ibid.*, p. 36.
5. *Ibid.*
6. J. L. Curry, p. 67 and I. Völgyes, p. 77, in Zoltán Bárány and Iván Völgyes, *The Legacies of Communism in Eastern Europe* (Baltimore: The Johns Hopkins University Press, 1955).
7. *Ibid.*, p. 58.
8. Völgyes, p. 14.
9. Curry, p. 70.
10. Rosenberg, p. 23.
11. *Ibid.*, p. 31.
12. *Ibid.*, p. 30.
13. *Ibid.*, p. 18.
14. B. Korvig, p. 35 in Bárány and Völgyes.
15. "T. Gurr" by J. L. Curry, p. 55 in Bárány and Völgyes.
16. Korvig, p. 15 in Bárány and Völgyes.

Bibliography

BOOKS

Bárány, Zoltán and Iván Völgyes. *The Legacies of Communism in Eastern Europe.* Baltimore: The Johns Hopkins University Press, 1995.

Beniak, Milan, and Miloslav Tichý. *Dejiny Lekárskej Fakulty Univerzity Komenského v Bratislave.* Bratislava: Univerzita Komenského, 1992.

Benke, J. *Medical University of Pécs: A Historical Review.* Pécs: University Press Pécs, 1991.

Čársky, Konštantín. *Chirurg Spomína.* Slovenské Spisovatel, 1987.

Encyklopédia Slovenska. Bratislava: VEDA, 1977-1981.

Gellner, Ernest. *Conditions of Liberty.* New York: The Penguin Press, 1994.

Graham, Loren R. *Science in Russia and the Soviet Union.* Cambridge University Press, 1993.

Hautová, Júlia. *Comenius University 1919–1994 Bratislava.* Bratislava: Comenius University, 1994.

Johnson, Owen V. *Slovakia 1918–1938: Education and the Making of the Nation.* New York: Columbia University Press, 1985.

Novomeský, Ladislav. *Desatročia do chvíľ skľbené: Jar v Pešti.* Bratislava: Smena, 1984.

Rosenbaum, Karol. *Ladislav Novomeský, 1904-1974.* Martin: Matica Slovenská, 1974.

Rosenberg, Tina. *The Haunted Land.* New York: Random House, 1995.

Rothstein, W. G. *American Medical Schools and the Practice of Medicine: A History.* New York: Oxford University Press, 1987.

Sečanský, Imrich. *Spomienky a Vyznanie Lekára.* Bratislava: Slovak Academic Press, 1997.

Seton-Watson, R. W. *Documents II. Ústav T. G. Masaryka.* Matica Slovenská, 1996.

Vrba, R. and Alan Bestic, *I Cannot Forget.* Sidwick and Jackson and Antony Gibbs and Phillips, 1963.

ARTICLES

Čársky, J., D. Hermanová, and M. Tichý. "Sto rokov od narodenia Prof. Ing. Dr. tech. Františka Valentiná." *Bratislavské Lekárske Listy* 93 (1992): 219-221.

Červaňanská, N. "Profesor K. Hynek a Spolok Slovenských Lekárov." *Bratislavské Lekárske Listy* 40 (1963): 368-371.

Československe Dejiny v datech. 1986: 609-613, 623-627.

Duránik, D. and E. Sedláčková. "Sto rokov od narodenia prvého slovenského profesora zubného lekarstva." *Nemocnica* 1 (1996): 26-27.

Halaga, O. R. "20 rokov Lekárskej Fakulty Univerzity P. J. Šafárika v Košiciach. 1948–1968." *Slovenské Pedagogické Nakladatelštvo* (Bratislava).

Horejší, J. "Vedecká osobnost profesora K. Hynka." *Bratislavské Lekárske Listy* 40 (1960): 371-375.

_____., "Vedecká osobnost profesora Kristiana Hynka, 1879–1960." *Čas. Lek. Šek.* 118 (1979): 1149-1152.

Inczinger, F. "K sedemdesiatinám Profesora Františka Šveca." *Čs. Farmacie* 15 (1966): 452.

Jurkovič, I. and R. Pospíšil. "K 45 výročiu založenia Lekárskej Fakulty Univerzity P. K. Šafárika." *Folia Fac. med. Safarikianae Cassoviensis* (1993) 1:9-15.

Kohút, A. and J. Lacko. "40 rokov Lekárskej Fakulty P. J. Šafárika." *Folia Fac. med. Safarikianae Cassoviensis* (1998) 1: 11-21.

Korec, R. "Prof. MUDr. Jozef Skotnický 80 ročný." *Bratislavské Lekárske Listy* 91 (1990): 739.

Kutlík, I. "História Vývoja Patologickej Anatomie na Slovensku." *Bratislavské Lekárske Listy* 42 (1962): 415-436.

_____. "K. polstoročnému výrociu smrti Júliusa A. Ladzianského." *Bratislavské Lekárske Listy* 94 (1993): 133-135.

Michalík, V. "Vysokoskolškré Requiem." *Svedectvo* 1 (1992):13-14.

Mikulecký, M. "Dérerov Objav Optikou Citačnej Analýzy." *Vesmír* 70 (1991); 276-277.

Mydlík, M. "Tradícia memoriálov Prof. MUDr. Frantiska Póra." *Vnitřní Lekařství* 22 (1998): 176-177.

Ondrejička, M. "K nedožitým devatdesiatinám akademika Ladislav Dérera." *Vnitřní Lekařství* 11 (1987): 1031-1035.

Palko, V. "O nefunkčnej hrubej čiare." *Sme/Smena* 3 (1997): 7.

Perino, F. R. "Egas Monis, Founder of Psychosurgery, Creator of Angiography." *Journal International of Coll. Surgery* 36 (1961): 261-272.

Pleva, J. and M. Tichý. "Vývin Lekárskej Fakulty Univerzity Komenského v rokoch 1919–1969." *50 rokov Univerzity Komenského* Ed. B. Varsík. Bratislava: Univerzita Komenského, 1969.

Porubský, J. "Profesor MUDr. Herman Krsek 70 ročný." *Lekársky Obzor* 16 (1967): 591-592.

Rapaport, J. "Krátky život «živé hmoty»." *Nauka z žizň* 9 (1988): 165-168.

Redakcia: "Prof. Dr František Klein šestdesiat ročný." *Bratislavské Lekárske Listy* 38 (1958): 441-442.

Ruttkay-Nedecký, I. "Koho som si naozaj vážil: Ladislava Dérer." *Vesmír* 69 (1990): 699-700.

Sečanský, I. "Akademik Ladislav Dérer." *Zdravie* 44 (1988): 6-7.

Sedlačková, E. "75 rokov Lekárskej Faculty Univerzity Komenského v Bratislave." *Recipe* 3 (1994): 37.

Švec, J. "Vysokoskolské Requiem." *Svedectvo* (1992) 3: 4.

Štúrová, B. "Osobnost prof. K. Hynka." *Bratislavské Lekárske Listy* 40 (1960): 366-368.

Tichý, M., K. Kapeller, J. Dedek, and E. Chandogová. "Pamiatke troch profesorov." *Čs. zdravotníctví* 34 (1986): 40-45.

Tichý, M. and I. Riečanský. "Osobnosť Akademika Dérera." *Čs. zdravotníctví* 35 (1937): 526-532.

Tichý, M., L. Pavlíková, A. Kapellerová, and A. Schmídová. "Pôsobenie profesora MUDr. Alojza Churu na Lekárskej Fakulty Univerzity Komenského v Bratislave." *Bratislavské Lekárske Listy* 93 (1992): 203-207.

Tlačova Agentúra Slovenskej Republiky. "Lustračný zákon na Slovensku už neplatí." *Sme/Smena* (1997) 3: 1.

Vívoda, M. "Založenie a začiatky Lekárskej Fakulty Univerzity Komenského v Bratislave." *Bratislavské Lekárske Listy* 44 (1964): 554-564.

"Zápisnice zo zasadania profesorského zboru 1938–1955." Archív Lekárskej Fakulty S. U. Bratislava.